Every day of the year through the years, something dramatic, significant, sad or controversial has taken place in the world of sports. Things start, stop, pause, come together, begin anew. THE SPORTS DATE BOOK will be a compendium of these events. It will go through the years from January 1 to December 31—interweaving the passing seasons and the changing scene of culture and sports.

But no matter what day it is—something special is always happening in the world of sports.

THE SPORTS DATE BOOK

HARVEY FROMMER

tempo
books

GROSSET & DUNLAP
A Filmways Company
Publishers • New York

THE SPORTS DATE BOOK

ACKNOWLEDGMENTS

This book came to be as the result of the efforts and assistance of a few treasured people. A thank you to Wendy Wallace (my editor) whose guidance, considerations and interests were made available to me. The team on the bench—my children—Jennifer, Freddy, Ian—you helped, too. And finally—my broadcasting friend, Lou Ross of WEVD—thank you for your interest and your help.

HF

DEDICATION

TO GERTRUDE KATZ, ("GRANNY"),
WITH MUCH LOVE

INTRODUCTION

Dates are the markers of our lives. They record births, deaths, anniversaries, dramatic events, good times and bad moments. For those of us who are sports fans, dates have a special significance. For the world of sports, though always changing, is anchored in the record book and the records are all locked into time.

There are many who still can remember where they were and how they felt when the announcement was made that the Dodgers of Brooklyn and the Giants of New York would move to California. Others recall their emotions when Joe Namath led the fledgling American Football League New York Jets to a Super Bowl win; when Pele retired; when Babe Ruth died; when Lou Brock broke Ty Cobb's season and then career record for stolen bases; when the Mets traded Tom Seaver to the Reds; when Joe DiMaggio's hitting streak was stopped at 56 or Pete Rose's concluded at 44. Most Americans remember the special time and the special emotions when the United States Olympic hockey team scored a stunning upset and won those gold medals.

This book is a selective sampler of some of the most significant dates and deeds in the history of sports. It contains a lot of firsts and lasts: the first Rose Bowl game; first Sun Bowl; first Super Bowl; first World Series game; first professional baseball game; first inter-league trade; first National Hockey League game; first million dollar sports gate; first black player in baseball, basketball, hockey; first black umpire and first umpire to wear glasses while working a game; first home run hit by Babe Ruth . . .

Other dates of "firsts" in sports include the first night game; first date the entire major league schedule was played at night; first unassisted triple play in history; first Kentucky Derby; first U.S. boxing match televised in color and a host of other TV and radio sports firsts.

Where there are beginnings, there are also endings—and the dates of many of these "final" things will be found in the pages of this book: Babe Ruth's final appearance at Yankee Stadium; the last home run that the Babe hit, that Ted Williams hit; the day baseball's color line was broken forever; the 12th and final no-hitter of Bob Feller's brilliant career; the final fight of Rocky Marciano's career and the final day of his life, and of Roberto Clemente, Nellie Fox, Walter Johnson, Jess Willard, Jack Dempsey, Branch Rickey, and so many others.

Anyone interested in sports also will be interested in the seasonal patterns of sports dates. Some events have certain days and sections of the calendar reserved almost exclusively: January 1 (New Year's Day) is a traditional time for college bowl games. The third Sunday in January is almost the exclusive preserve of the National Football League's ultimate game—the Super Bowl.

April conjures up baseball and baseball dates; May has always been the month of the Kentucky Derby and Memorial Day—the time of the Indianapolis 500.

September and October are busy months for sports dates: the baseball pennant races leading up to the World Series vie for dates with golf, with the start of the basketball and football seasons and nowadays the ending of the professional soccer schedule. November is a time when baseball is out of the sports dates business, at least on the playing level, and hockey joins with basketball and football for a share of the action. And with December—and the end of a sports year—college basketball and football wind down and clamor for their share of sports dates . . . and the cycle repeats itself.

A close look at the dates of sports enables one to see some of the coincidences and ironies that time can create.

April 15, 1915—Jack Johnson became the first black heavyweight champion of the world. On that date thirty-two years later, Jackie Robinson broke major league baseball's color line. Robinson was four years old when Johnson won his championship. And Lew Alcindor (Kareem Abdul-Jabbar) was one-day-old the day after Jackie Robinson broke the color line. The great NBA center was born in New York City the day after Robinson's historic feat.

Babe Ruth and Willie Mays share May 6th. On that day in 1916, Babe Ruth hit his first major league home run. On that day in 1931, Willie Mays was born. Roger Bannister also has a share of May 6th. In 1954, he became the first person in history to run a mile in under four minutes.

Babe Ruth and Willie Mays also share May 25th. On that day in 1935, Ruth hit his final home run

#714. On the same day in 1951, the New York Giants called up a kid outfielder who was hitting .477 for their Minneapolis farm team. His name was Willie Howard Mays.

Days in June had a great deal of significance for Yankee immortal Lou Gehrig: He was born on June 19, 1903; he played in the first of his 2,130 record-setting consecutive games on June 1, 1925; he whacked four home runs on June 3, 1932; he died on June 2, 1941.

The 17th of July has a lot of significance for baseball fans: Ty Cobb died on this day, as did Dizzy Dean. And Joe DiMaggio's 56-game-hitting streak was stopped on a July 17th. In 1954, the Brooklyn Dodgers fielded a team that had more black players than whites; it had never happened before in baseball history.

But no matter what day it is—something special is always happening in the world of sports. As Casey Stengel used to say—"You can look it up . . ." I hope you enjoy looking it up as much as I did!

Harvey Frommer
June 15, 1980

JANUARY

January 1, 1897—The first black collegiate football game was played. Atlanta University defeated Tuskegee Institute at Atlanta, Georgia.

January 1, 1902—The University of Michigan defeated Stanford, 49–0, in the first Tournament of Roses football game at Pasadena, California.

January 1, 1911—Hank Greenberg was born in New York City. He would play thirteen years in the major leagues, be dubbed "Hammerin' Hank" because of his home run power and be admitted in 1956 to the Hall of Fame.

January 1, 1916—Washington State trimmed Brown University, 14–0 in the first of the continuing Rose Bowl games.

January 1, 1925—Notre Dame defeated Stanford, 27–10, in the Rose Bowl. The "Four Horsemen" backfield of Notre Dame played together for the last time.

January 1, 1923—"Wee Willie" Keeler died in Brooklyn, New York. Keeler played major league baseball for nineteen years. He recorded a lifetime batting average of .345 while swinging a bat that weighed only thirty ounces. In 1939, the man who "hit 'em where they ain't" was admitted into the Hall of Fame.

January 1, 1929—In Houston, Texas, Atlanta University's football team defeated Prairie View, 6–0. It was called "the Prairie View Game," and it was the first black college bowl game ever played.

January 1, 1929—Roy Riegels gained enduring sports notoriety. He ran 69 yards the "wrong way" as Georgia Tech defeated California, 8–7, in the Rose Bowl.

January 1, 1935—The first Sugar Bowl game was played. Tulane edged Temple, 20–14, at New Orleans, Louisiana.

January 1, 1935—The first Sun Bowl game was played at El Paso, Texas. Hardin Simmons University and New Mexico State played to a 14–14 tie.

January 1, 1937—The first Cotton Bowl game was played. TCU was a 16–6 victor over Marquette at Dallas, Texas.

January 1, 1946—The first Gator Bowl game was played. Wake Forest triumphed, 26–14, over South Carolina at Jacksonville, Florida.

January 1, 1947—Illinois defeated UCLA, 45–14, in the Rose Bowl. Buddy Young of the Illni became the first black player to score a touchdown in the Rose Bowl.

January 1, 1954—One of the strangest moments in the history of college football took place. At the Cotton Bowl, before more than 75,000 fans, Dicky Moegle of Rice was the victim of a "twelfth man" tackle. Alabama's Tommy Lewis came off the bench to knock down the Rice halfback as he ran toward the goal line. Moegle and Rice were awarded a touchdown which, at that point in the game, gave them a 14–6 lead. Rice won the game 28–6. Moegle racked up 264 yards and the Most Valuable Player award.

January, 1961—The first American Football League championship game was played. The Houston Oilers defeated Los Angeles, 24–16, before 32,183 people at Houston.

January 2, 1957—Gene Fullmer defeated Sugar Ray Robinson to win the middleweight boxing title.

January 2, 1965—The New York Jets signed Joe Namath to a $400,000 contract. Broadway Joe became the highest priced rookie in the history of pro football.

January 3, 1939—Bobby Hull was born. He would be a National Hockey League All-Star ten times, win the NHL goal scoring title seven times and win the scoring championship three times. Hull has been called the fastest player on ice—he was clocked at 29.7 miles per hour in his prime.

After the 1971–72 season, Hull became player-coach of the Winnipeg Jets of the World Hockey Association. A new league and a new team gave him the nickname "the Golden Jet". The "Golden" some said came from the ten-year contract he signed that totaled almost three-million dollars, a third of which came when he inked his new contract.

January 3, 1973—CBS sold the New York Yankees for ten million dollars to George Steinbrenner and eleven other members of a syndicate.

January 4, 1930—Don Shula, who would become one of the top coaches in the National Football League, was born.

January 4, 1930—Floyd Patterson, who would grow up to become heavyweight boxing champion, was born in Brooklyn.

January 4, 1968—This was the birth date of the North American Soccer League. It resulted from a merger of the United Soccer Association (USA) and the National Professional Soccer League (NPSL). The USA and the NPSL had been formed in 1967—one backed by the United States Soccer Federation and the Federation International de Football (soccer's world ruling body), the other (NPSL) buttressed by CBS television exposure. The 1967 season was a disaster for both leagues they lost a lot of money, which paved the way for merger negotiations. Seventeen franchises began the first season of the

North American Soccer League; a dozen collapsed. Only Atlanta, Baltimore, Dallas, Kansas City and St. Louis remained to compete in 1969 —the NASL's second season.

January 5, 1920—Babe Ruth, a pitcher-outfielder, was sold by the Boston Red Sox to the New York Yankees for $125,000. Yankee owner Jacob Ruppert also provided the Red Sox with a Fenway Park mortgage of $350,000.

January 5, 1932—Chuck Noll, who would lead the Pittsburgh Steelers to dominance in the National Football League, was born.

January 5, 1934—A uniform baseball was selected for use by both the National and American Leagues. It was the first time in thirty-three years that players in both leagues used the same baseball.

January 5, 1963—Baseball Hall of Famer Rogers Hornsby died in Chicago at the age of 66. Hornsby had a lifetime batting average of .358 and batted .400 three times.

January 5, 1975—Don Wilson of the Houston Astros and his son were found dead of carbon monoxide poisoning at their family home. Wilson had pitched two no-hitters for the Astros.

January 6, 1920—This was the birth date of Early Wynn who would win over 300 games in his career as a star pitcher in the major leagues.

January 6, 1921—Gary Middlecoff was born; thirty-four years later he would win the Masters Golf Tournament.

January 7, 1922—Alvin Dark was born. In 1948, he would win the National League's Rookie-of-the-Year award.

January 7, 1930—Eddie Le Baron was born. He would grow up to star in the National Football League.

January 7, 1950—The South defeated the North, 22–13, in the first Senior Bowl football game ever played.

January 7, 1962—The West defeated the East, 47–27, in the first American Football League All-Star game before a crowd of 20,973 at San Diego.

January 8, 1957—Jackie Robinson announced his retirement from baseball. The man who broke baseball's color line stated in a *Look Magazine* article that he would become a Chock full o' Nuts vice president.

January 9, 1934—Bart Starr, who would become one of the great quarterbacks in Green Bay Packer history, was born.

January 9, 1951—It was announced that Boston Red Sox slugger Ted Williams would be called back into the Marine Corps to join other major leaguers involved in the Korean War.

January 10, 1949—This was the birth date of George Foreman, who would become heavyweight boxing champion.

January 11, 1890—One of baseball's greatest base stealers, Max Carey, was born in Terre Haute, Indiana.

January 11, 1960—Dolph Schayes of the Syracuse Nats became the first player in NBA history to score 15,000 points. Schayes recorded his 15,013th point in a game against the Boston Celtics.

January 11, 1964—Bud Wilkinson ended a 17-year reign by resigning as Oklahoma's head football coach.

January 11, 1970—The fourth Super Bowl was played before 80,562 at Tulane Stadium, New Orleans. Kansas City defeated Minnesota, 23–7. The gross receipts of approximately $3.8-million were the largest ever for a one-day team sports event. It was estimated that the TV audience was the largest to that point in history for a one-day sports event.

January 11, 1973—Baseball's "designated hitter" was born. The American League was given permission to allow a player to bat in place of the pitcher while allowing the pitcher to remain in the game.

January 12, 1969—A 24-year-old quarterback named Joe Namath led the New York Jets of the

American Football Conference to a 16–7 win over the Baltimore Colts of the National Football Conference in the third Super Bowl. A cocky Namath had predicted a Jet victory and made good on his promise.

January 13, 1933—Tom Gola was born. In 1955, he would come out of LaSalle College to star in the National Basketball Association.

January 14, 1954—In a marriage out of Hollywood casting, Yankee immortal Joe DiMaggio married Marilyn Monroe. "It's got to be better than rooming with Joe Page," DiMaggio cracked when asked how he felt about the marriage.

January 14, 1968—The first three-million-dollar gate in the history of pro football was achieved. Green Bay defeated Oakland, 33–14, in the second Super Bowl staged at Miami's Orange Bowl.

January 14, 1978—Joe McCarthy died. A long-time baseball manager, he led the New York Yankees to eight American League pennants from 1931 to 1946.

January 15, 1911—Jerome Herman Dean was born in a rickety shack on a plot of Arkansas ground that his destitute sharecropper parents worked. He would be better known as "Dizzy Dean," star pitcher for the St. Louis Cardinals and one of the most colorful characters in baseball history. As a youth, Dizzy picked cotton for fifty cents a day. Although he bragged that he learned about pitching while attending Oklahoma State Teachers College, he only went as far as the second grade in his schooling. Dean grew to be a 6'2", slope-shouldered right-hander. He summarized his pitching strategy in these words: "I never bothered what those guys could hit and couldn't hit. All I knowed is that they weren't gonna get a-holt of that ball ol' Diz was throwin'."

January 15, 1942—President Franklin D. Roosevelt sent what would be known as his "Green Letter" to baseball Commissioner Landis. FDR said that despite the United States battling in World War II, "I honestly think it would be best for the country to keep baseball going."

January 15, 1965—In one of the most shocking trades in the history of sports, Wilt Chamberlain was acquired by the Philadelphia 76ers from San Francisco. The Warriors obtained three average players and an undisclosed sum of money.

January 15, 1967—The first Super Bowl was played. The Green Bay Packers defeated the Kansas City Chiefs, 35–10. The first Super Bowl was the first dual-network color coverage simulcast of a sports event in history and attracted the largest viewership ever to witness a sporting event up to that time. The Nielsen rating indicated that 73 million fans watched all or part of that game on one of the two networks, CBS or NBC. In actuality, the game was a contest between the two leagues and the two networks, for the CBS allegiance was to the NFL, and the NBC loyalty was to the American Football

League, which it had virtually created with its network dollars.

January 15, 1968—Bill Masterson became the first player to die as a result of an injury sustained in a National Hockey League game. Masterson of the Minnesota North Stars, died of a brain injury incurred in a game two days earlier against the Oakland Seals.

January 15, 1978—Dallas defeated Denver, 27–10, in Super Bowl XII. It was the first Super Bowl ever staged indoors. The game played at the Superdome in New Orleans was watched by 102,010,000—and was estimated to be the largest TV viewership for a show of this type at this point in history.

January 16, 1905—Ottawa defeated Dawson City, 23–2, in a game that featured the most goals ever scored in a pro hockey game.

January 16, 1935—This was the birth date of champion racing car driver A.J. Foyt.

January 16, 1972—In Super Bowl VI Dallas defeated Miami, 24–3, at Tulane Stadium, New Orleans. The telecast of the game drew the largest viewership for a one-day event at this point in history.

January 17, 1837—This was the birth date of William Curtis, acknowledged to be the "father" of American amateur sports and American rowing.

January 17, 1916—New York City was the site of the formation of the Professional Golfers' Association of America.

January 17, 1929—Jacques Plante was born. He was destined to become one of hockey's outstanding goalies.

January 18, 1942—Cassius Clay, who would become better known as Muhammad Ali, was born.

January 18, 1967—Two storied sports figures died. "Goose" Tatum, longtime star for the Harlem Globetrotters and Barney Ross, onetime lightweight and welterweight boxing champ, passed away.

January 19, 1952—The franchise of the New York Yankees football team was purchased for $300,000 by the NFL and transferred to Dallas.

January 20, 1940—Carol Heiss, who would win the 1960 Olympic women's singles figure skating championship, was born.

January 20, 1966—Ted Williams was elected to baseball's Hall of Fame.

January 20, 1968—UCLA with Lew Alcindor (Kareem Abdul-Jabbar) opposed Houston with Elvin Hayes before a crowd of 52,693 at the Astrodome. UCLA had been unbeaten for the past two years; the last time Houston had lost was against UCLA the season before. Hayes scored 39 to lead his Houston team to a 71–69 upset victory. Alcindor was held to fifteen points. And UCLA's 47-game winning streak was stopped.

January 20, 1978—Dit Clapper, who starred for twenty years with the Boston Bruins of the National Hockey League, died.

January 20, 1980—The Pittsburgh Steelers defeated the Los Angeles Rams, 31–19, at the Rose Bowl in Pasadena, California. More than 100,000 attended the 14th Super Bowl—the largest crowd in the history of the event. Terry Bradshaw became the first quarterback to win four Super Bowls.

January 21, 1888—The United States Amateur Athletic Union was created.

January 21, 1940—This was the birth date of golfing great Jack Nicklaus.

January 21, 1969—The twenty-second National Hockey League All-Star game was played. For the first time, a Western Division squad opposed an Eastern Division team. Claude Larose of Minnesota scored with less than three minutes remaining in the game to give the West a 3–3 tie over the heavily-favored East.

January 22, 1962—Two new inductees to baseball's Hall of Fame were Bob Feller and Jackie Robinson. Besides becoming the first black to play major league baseball, Robinson was also the first black to be admitted to the Hall of Fame.

January 22, 1973—With his defeat of Joe Frazier, George Foreman became the new heavyweight boxing champion.

January 23, 1933—Baseball's Pacific Coast League established minimum prices for bleacher and grandstand seats for the 1933 season. Bleacher seats were fixed at 25 cents; grandstand locations at 40 cents.

January 24, 1870—William Morgan, who twenty years later would create the sport of volleyball, was born.

January 24, 1969—Former Washington Senator pitcher Tom Zachary died. Zachary is remembered as the pitcher who threw the pitch that Babe Ruth pounded for his 60th home run of the 1927 season.

January 25, 1924—Lou ("the toe") Groza was born. He would play for twenty-one years in the National Football League and score 1,608 points.

January 25, 1945—Larry MacPhail teamed with Dan Topping and Del Webb to purchase the New York Yankees for $2.8 million.

January 25, 1968—A new indoor pole vault world record was set by Bob Seagren. He cleared 17 feet, 4¼ inches in the Milrose Games at New York's Madison Square Garden.

January 26, 1871—London, England was the site of the formation of the Rugby Football

Union. The organization was formed to distinguish the sport from football (soccer).

January 26, 1951—Jimmy Foxx and Mel Ott were elected to baseball's Hall of Fame.

January 26, 1955—Joe DiMaggio, the Yankee Clipper, was elected to baseball's Hall of Fame.

January 26, 1960—Pete Rozelle, who did publicity work for the Los Angeles Rams, was chosen as the new National Football League Commissioner.

January 26, 1965—Harry Stuhldreher, famed quarterback member of Notre Dame's "Four Horsemen," passed away.

January 26, 1970—On the tenth anniversary of his becoming National Football League Commissioner, Pete Rozelle made public the signing of a record $124,000,000 TV football deal. The three networks obtained rights to televise pre and regular season games, playoff games and the Super Bowl.

January 27, 1937—Cy Young and Tris Speaker were elected to the Hall of Fame in the second Cooperstown shrine induction.

January 28, 1932—This was the birth date of Parry O'Brien, who would become one of the greatest of all shotputters.

January 28, 1957—Throughout most of their

seasons in Brooklyn, the Dodgers were affectionately referred to as "Bums" by their fans. On this date in the last year of the team, the Dodgers signed Emmett Kelly, a clown, who starred for many years with the Ringling Brothers Barnum and Bailey Circus. He was put under contract to entertain at Dodger games.

January 28, 1958—The career of star catcher Roy Campanella was ended. The great Dodger leader was injured in an automobile accident and confined to a wheelchair for the rest of his life.

January 28, 1977—Jack Manders died. He was a place-kicking specialist who earned the nickname "Automatic Jack." Manders was a big reason for the undefeated season of his Chicago Bears teammates in 1934.

January 29, 1878—Barney Oldfield, whose name would become a synonym for auto racing and who would become the first to move a car a mile a minute, was born.

January 29, 1900—This was the birth date of baseball's American League. The charter members of the "junior circuit" were: Chicago, Boston, Detroit, Philadelphia, Baltimore, Washington, Cleveland, Milwaukee. The new league was aided by players who had "jumped" from the National League. Nap Lajoie came to the Philadelphia Athletics from the Phillies, batted .422 to win the batting title, drove in 125 runs to win the RBI crown, and slammed 14 home runs to win the home run championship. Cy Young came

over from St. Louis and won 33 games for Boston
—tops in the league. The new clubs in Boston
and Chicago would outdraw the established
teams in those National League cities during the
American League's first season.

January 29, 1936—Baseball's Hall of Fame
elected its first members: Ty Cobb, Walter Johnson, Christy Mathewson, Babe Ruth and Honus
Wagner.

January 30, 1973—The first National Hockey
League All-Star game ever staged at Madison
Square Garden took place. The East defeated the
West, 5–4. The largest crowd to that point in All-
Star hockey competition saw Greg Polis emerge
as the star of the game. Polis scored two goals
and was voted the game's Most Valuable Player
award. It was a nice reward for Polis who arrived
only hours before game time following the birth
of his first child in Pittsburgh.

January 31, 1913—Don Hutson, one of pro
football's great pass receivers and a member of
the Hall of Fame, was born.

January 31, 1914—Jersey Joe Walcott was born.
He would become the heavyweight champion of
the world thirty-seven years later.

January 31, 1919—Jackie Roosevelt Robinson
was born in Cairo, Georgia. In 1947, this grandson of slaves would break baseball's color line.

January 31, 1931—Two-time National League

Most Valuable Player Ernie Banks was born in Dallas, Texas. Banks played nineteen years for the Chicago Cubs and was admitted to baseball's Hall of Fame in 1977. He recorded 512 career home runs.

January 31, 1947—Nolan Ryan was born in Refugio, Texas. He would grow up to be a 6'-2", fireballing pitcher.

FEBRUARY

February 1, 1895—George "Papa" Bear, one-time coach and owner of the Chicago Bears of the National Football League, was born.

February 1, 1968—On this day, famed golfer Lawson Little died.

February 2, 1876—Professional baseball's senior loop—the National League—was created. The eight charter teams were Chicago, Boston, New York, Philadelphia, Hartford, St. Louis, Cincinnati, and Louisville.

February 2, 1918—The world of boxing lost one of its most colorful characters and great champions. John L. Sullivan died.

February 2, 1967—This was the birth date of the American Basketball Association—a league that used a red, white and blue basketball and featured the three-point shot.

February 3, 1939—Charles ("Cash and Carry") Pyle died. He was one of the legendary sports promoters. Dance marathons, six-day bike races, tennis exhibitions and the contracting of Red

Grange to play at $3,000 a game were among his accomplishments. Pyle agreed with P.T. Barnum that "there's a sucker born every minute." Pyle ran his business affairs with money on an up-front basis, and that's how his nickname came about.

February 3, 1940—Fran Tarkenton, one of the great scrambling quarterbacks in NFL history, was born.

February 3, 1945—Bob Griese was born. He would lead the Miami Dolphins to power and prestige in the NFL.

February 3, 1972—Sapporo, Japan was the site of the first Winter Olympics held in Asia.

February 4, 1932—Lake Placid, New York was the site of the first United States Winter Olympic Games.

February 4, 1952—Jackie Robinson of the Brooklyn Dodgers recorded another first. He was appointed director of communication activities for NBC's New York radio and TV stations. He thus became the first black executive to hold a post of that nature.

February 5, 1934—Hank Aaron was born in Mobile, Alabama. He would become a member of the Milwaukee Braves in 1954 and in 1974, would hit his 715th home run breaking Babe Ruth's record. Retiring from baseball in 1976, Hank ranked first in games played, times at bat, home runs, and runs batted in.

February 5, 1942—Roger Staubach, great Dallas Cowboys quarterback, was born.

February 7, 1959—Nap Lajoie died in Daytona Beach, Florida. Admitted to baseball's Hall of Fame in 1937, he batted .339 as a 21-year career average.

February 6, 1895—George Herman Ruth, best known as "the Babe," was born in Baltimore, Maryland.

February 7, 1969—Diane Crump became the first woman to compete as a jockey in a regular race at a major track. She finished tenth aboard Bridle 'N' Bit.

February 7, 1973—Monte Irvin was elected to baseball's Hall of Fame.

February 8, 1936—The first National Football League draft in history took place. The first selection was made by the Philadelphia Eagles. They chose Jay Berwanger.

February 9, 1895—The Minnesota State School of Agriculture defeated Hamline College, 9–3, in the first college basketball game ever played.

February 9, 1907—Future hockey Hall of Famer Audrey "Dit" Clapper was born. For twenty years he would wear number 5 on the back of his Boston Bruins uniform.

February 10, 1893—Future tennis great Bill Tilden was born. He would become the first

American to win a men's singles championship at Wimbledon.

February 10, 1915—Allie Reynolds was born in Bethany, Oklahoma. He was a star pitcher for thirteen seasons with the Cleveland Indians and New York Yankees. Known as "Superchief" because of his Indian descent, he pitched two no-hitters in 1951.

February 10, 1950—Mark Spitz was born. He would win seven gold medals for swimming in the 1972 Olympics.

February 10, 1962—Jim Beatty became the first American to break the four minute barrier for an indoor mile. Beatty recorded a time of 3:58.9 in a Los Angeles meet.

February 11, 1949—The world featherweight boxing title once again belonged to Willie Pep. He defeated Sandy Saddler in a title fight in New York City.

February 11, 1973—Shane Gould became the first woman to swim the 1500-meter freestyle in less than seventeen seconds.

February 11, 1977—The San Francisco Giants sent infielders Bill Madlock and Rob Sperring to the Chicago Cubs for Bobby Murcer, Steve Ontiveros and a minor league pitcher.

February 12, 1917—Dom DiMaggio, a younger brother of Hall of Famer Joe, was born in San

Francisco. Dom would play for the Boston Red Sox from 1940–1953 and record a lifetime batting average of .298.

February 12, 1926—Joe Garagiola was born in St. Louis. His lifetime batting average over a nine year major league career was .257. His greatest fame was to come as a humorous and knowledgeable TV sportscaster.

February 12, 1934—Bill Russell was born. He would become one of the greatest defensive players in the history of the National Basketball Association and win the MVP award five times.

February 13, 1965—The United States ladies senior figure skating championship was won by Peggy Fleming at Lake Placid, New York.

February 14, 1941—Frank Leahy was appointed as Notre Dame's head football coach.

February 14, 1951—Sugar Ray Robinson became the world middleweight boxing champion. He defeated Jake LaMotta in a title bout in Chicago. It was the first time that a welterweight champion defeated a middleweight champion.

February 15, 1914—John Melvin Hill was born. In 1936, he became a member of the Boston Bruins of the National Hockey League. He lasted through the 1945–46 season as a journeyman forward and would have gone through his career unnoticed if it had not been for the touch of greatness that seized him in the 1939 Stanley

Cup playoffs. In the opening game of the final series, Boston was tied, 1–1, with the New York Rangers. There were only thirty-five seconds left in the third overtime (sudden death) period. Speeding down the right side, Hill snared a pass from teammate Bill Cowley and shot the puck into the Ranger goal. Hill scored another sudden-death goal in the second game. The score was tied in the ninth minute of the first overtime when Hill got off a thirty-foot shot that evaded Ranger goalie Bert Gardiner. The series moved to a seventh and decisive game. The teams once again battled through regulation time, through the first overtime, the second overtime. At approximately one o'clock in the morning—eight minutes into the third overtime period—Hill struck again. He smashed the goal in for Boston's winning score. Thus, Hill scored goals in three different overtime games, including the seventh game's third overtime period ... and earned fame and the nickname "Sudden Death Mell Hill."

February 15, 1953—Victories at Davos, Switzerland made Tenley Albright the first American woman to hold the world figure skating championship.

February 15, 1980—Wayne Getzky of the Edmonton Oilers tied one National Hockey League record and set another in his team's 8–2 defeat of the Washington Capitols. The nineteen-year-old Gretzky, who signed a twenty-one-year contract with the Oilers in 1979, equalled a league mark with seven assists. He also moved his season scoring total to 96, setting a new rookie record.

February 16, 1972—Wilt "the Stilt" Chamberlain, a four-time Most Valuable Player and the greatest offensive threat in the history of the National Basketball Association, became the first player in history to score 30,000 points in a career.

February 17, 1968—Basketball's Hall of Fame began operations at Springfield College in Springfield, Massachusetts, near the site where James Naismith invented the sport.

February 18, 1970—Pitcher Denny McLain was suspended from baseball for two years. Commissioner Bowie Kuhn ordered the suspension because of McLain's alleged involvement in book-making ventures.

February 19, 1953—Boston Red Sox slugger Ted Williams, battling in the Korean War, safely crash landed his crippled panther jet after a combat mission.

February 20, 1952—Emmett Ashford became organized baseball's first black umpire. Ashford was given an opportunity as a substitute umpire in the Southwestern International League.

February 21, 1977—Former Green Bay Packer tackle Henry Jordan died. A star in the 1960's, he said of his coach Vince Lombardi: "He treats us very fair—all the same—like dogs."

February 21, 1980—Speed skater Eric Heiden became the first Olympic athlete to ever win five individual gold medals. Heiden won the men's

10,000-meter speed skating competition and set a new world and olympic record for the time. Heiden's other medals in the XIII Olympic Games were picked up for 500-meter, 1,000-meter, 1,500-meter and 5,000-meter speed skating.

February 22, 1957—A second round kayo of Johnny Saxton in Cleveland enabled Carmen Basilio to retain the welterweight boxing title.

February 22, 1969—Barbara Jo Rubin became the first woman jockey to win a race. Ms. Rubin aboard Cohesian won by a neck in the historic Charles Town, West Virginia race.

February 22, 1980—The United States hockey team scored one of the greatest upsets in sports history by defeating the Soviet Union, 4–3, in the Olympic Games at Lake Placid, New York. Russia had won the gold medal in the four previous ice hockey competitions in the Olympics. The American victory was a triumph of amateurs over professionals. The team from the Soviet Union had defeated a National Hockey League All-Star squad, the New York Rangers, the New York Islanders, and less than two weeks before the U.S. Olympic hockey team in an exhibition game at Madison Square Garden.

February 23, 1941—Ron Hunt was born in St. Louis, Missouri. In 1963, he began his major league baseball career with the New York Mets. Hunt was a scrappy, determined player. He was hit by more pitches than any other player in the history of baseball. In one season Hunt reached base fifty times as a result of being hit by pitches.

February 23, 1960—A two-ton ball caved in the roof of the visiting dugout at Ebbets Field. It was one of the first stages in the demolition of the ballpark to ready the site for a housing project.

February 24, 1874—Honus Wagner was born in Carnegie, Pennsylvania. He would play in the major leagues for twenty-one seasons, stroke 3430 hits, steal 722 bases, drive in 1732 runs and record a lifetime batting average of .328. In 1936, he would be admitted into baseball's Hall of Fame.

February 24, 1980—One of the most stunning moments in American sports history took place at the XIIIth Olympic Games at Lake Placid. The United States hockey team defeated Finland, 4–3 to win the gold medal. A foot-stomping, flag-waving audience at the Olympic Field House cheered on the young American team. All over the United States, cries of "We're No. 1," and "USA" were heard. The contest began on a Sunday morning at 11:00, and millions changed their weekend routine to watch the "Miracle at Lake Placid," a victory that seemed impossible when the Olympics began. It was only the second gold medal won by an American hockey team in Olympic history. Twenty years before, a U.S. team won the ice hockey championship at Squaw Valley, California. "I'm sure the twenty guys can't believe it," said Mark Johnson of the U.S. win. Johnson had scored the final goal for the U.S. "They'll probably wake up tomorrow," Johnson said, "and still won't believe it."

February 25, 1940—The first telecast of an American hockey game was transmitted over station W2XBS in New York City. The viewing audience watched the New York Rangers battle the Montreal Canadiens at Madison Square Garden.

February 25, 1964—Muhammad Ali, known then as Cassius Clay, defeated Sonny Liston and became heavyweight boxing champion of the world.

February 26, 1887—Grover Cleveland Alexander was born in Elba, Nebraska. Twenty-four years later he would win twenty-eight games as a rookie pitcher for the Philadelphia Phillies.

February 26, 1935—Babe Ruth was released by the New York Yankees and signed by the Boston Braves.

February 27, 1874—At Lord's Cricket Ground, the first baseball game in England was played. The teams were composed of English soccer and cricket players plus a few baseball players from the United States.

February 27, 1959—The Boston Celtics scored 173 points against Minneapolis—the most points ever scored by one team in a National Basketball Association game.

February 28, 1940—Collegiate basketball was televised for the first time. Station W2XBS transmitted a basketball doubleheader from Madison Square Garden. Pittsburgh played Fordham and New York University competed against Georgetown.

February 28, 1960—The Soviet Union wound up as the unofficial team champion of the 1960 Winter Olympics held at Squaw Valley in California.

February 29, 1904—Pepper Martin was born in Temple, Oklahoma. Twenty-four years later he would begin an exciting thirteen-year career with the St. Louis Cardinals.

February 29, 1980—Gordie Howe of the Hartford Whalers recorded his 800th goal in regular season National Hockey League play. The 51-year-old Howe became the first player in NHL history to reach that mark. Howe's score came on a wrist shot from ten feet out that put the puck between the pads of Mike Liut, St. Louis Blues goalie.

MARCH

March 1, 1968—Elvin Hayes of Houston was selected by the Associated Press as the collegiate player of the year.

March 1, 1969—Mickey Mantle retired from baseball after an eighteen-year career with the New York Yankees. Five years later he would be admitted to the Hall of Fame.

March 1, 1980—Emmett Ashford, major league baseball's first black umpire, died of a heart attack in Los Angeles. He was 66 years old. An umpire for twenty years, the final five in the American League, Ashford retired in 1970. He was a theatrical type performer whose loud voice and animated gestures entertained fans.

March 2, 1927—Babe Ruth signed a three-year contract with the New York Yankees. The Babe's $70,000 a year pact made him then the highest paid player in baseball.

March 2, 1951—Boston Garden was the site of the first All-Star game in National Basketball Association history. The East defeated the West, 111–94, before 10,094. "Easy Ed" Macauley was the game's high scorer with twenty points and was voted the Most Valuable Player award.

March 2, 1962—Wilt Chamberlain set an all-time NBA record by scoring 100 points in Philadelphia's 169–147 victory over New York in a game played at Hershey, Pennsylvania. The game also marked the most points ever scored by two teams in the NBA (316). Chamberlain's scoring came on 36 out of 63 field-goal attempts and 28 of 32 free throw attempts.

March 2, 1970—Paul Christman, a top former football player and an admired sportscaster, died.

March 3, 1872—William Henry Keeler was born in Brooklyn, New York. Keeler, who would be better known as "Wee Willie," grew up to be just 5'4" and 140 pounds. Pound for pound and inch for inch he would become one of the great players in baseball history.

March 3, 1959—The San Francisco Giants named their ballpark "Candlestick Park."

March 4, 1970—A 101–97 victory by Jacksonville University over Miami U. climaxed the victor's historic season. Jacksonville became the first major college basketball team to average better than 100 points a game.

March 5, 1918—Paul Christman, who would become a top collegiate and professional football player, was born.

March 5, 1965—Pepper Martin died. Dubbed "The Wild Horse of the Osage," he was a star for the St. Louis Cardinals in the 1930's. He could hit, he could run, he could throw, he could win. He did all of these things with an abandon that helped earn him his nickname. If he could not stop a hard smash down to his third-base position with his glove, he would stop the ball with his chest. Three times during the 1930's, he led the National League in stolen bases, and throughout that decade he was the 'horse' that led the Cardinal 'Gashouse Gang.'

March 6, 1940—Willie Stargell was born in Earlsboro, Oklahoma. Twenty-two years later he would begin an illustrious career with the Pittsburgh Pirates.

March 6, 1976—"Slapsie Maxie" Rosenbloom died. Elected to boxing's Hall of Fame in 1972, he was a former light-heavyweight boxing champion who achieved additional fame in his movie career.

March 7, 1950—Pittsburgh Steeler star Franco Harris was born.

March 7, 1950—James Rodney Richard was born at Vienna, Louisiana. He would grow up to be a 6'-8", 200-pound hard-throwing right-handed pitcher for the Houston Astros.

March 7, 1954—In its first international ice hockey competition, the Soviet Union defeated Canada in Sweden to claim the world title.

March 7, 1977—Bernie Bierman died. A University of Minnesota coach from 1932 to 1950, he led his teams to three national championships.

March 8, 1922—Carl Furillo, who would star for fifteen years as a member of the Brooklyn Dodgers, was born in Stony Creek Mills, Pennsylvania.

March 8, 1971—A record gross for an indoor fight was set as Joe Frazier defeated Muhammad Ali at Madison Square Garden to win the heavyweight championship of the world.

March 9, 1948—Billy Taylor of the New York Rangers and Don Gallinger of the Boston Bruins were suspended for life by the National Hockey League for alleged gambling ties.

March 10, 1941—It was announced that all members of the Brooklyn Dodgers would be wearing batting helmets. Dodger general manager Larry MacPhail said that the helmets invented by surgeons at Johns Hopkins would ultimately be worn by all major league ballplayers.

March 10, 1958—Rocky Marciano rejected an offer in excess of one million dollars to give up his retirement and fight Floyd Patterson for boxing's heavyweight championship.

March 11, 1882—This was the organizational birth date of the Intercollegiate Lacrosse Association.

March 12, 1966—A new hockey record for points scored in one season was set when Bobby Hull of Chicago scored his 51st point in a game against the Rangers.

March 12, 1973—Hall of Famer Frankie Frisch, the "Fordham Flash," died at the age of 72.

March 12, 1980—Chuck Klein and Tom Yawkey were admitted posthumously to the baseball Hall of Fame. Chosen by the veterans committee, which offers a second chance to candidates not selected by writers, Klein and Yawkey varied in their baseball accomplishments. Klein was a seventeen-year National League veteran who pounded three hundred home runs. Yawkey, former owner of the Boston Red Sox, built the organization into one of baseball's top franchises by spending money freely to acquire top players.

March 13, 1886—John Franklin Baker was born in Trappe, Maryland. Baker grew up to become an athlete known as "Home Run Baker." If there was ever a ballplayer who became a legend because of a nickname, it had to be Baker. In his thirteen-year playing career with the Philadelphia Athletics and New York Yankees, the left-handed batter collected a grand total of just ninety-three homers. His best home run year was 1913, when he popped twelve round-trippers. Baker was admitted to baseball's Hall of Fame in 1955.

March 13, 1960—The Chicago Cardinals franchise of the National Football League was transferred to St. Louis.

March 14, 1925—Walter Camp, acknowledged as the originator of the concept of the All-American football team, died.

March 14, 1967—Bubba Smith, a defensive lineman from Michigan State, was the first player chosen in the first combined player selections of the NFL and AFL. Smith was picked by the Baltimore Colts.

March 14, 1972—The Cincinnati Royals of the National Basketball Association announced that the team's franchise would be shifted to Kansas City, Missouri at the end of the season.

March 15, 1869—The Cincinnati Red Stockings, baseball's first professional team, was formed. The stars of the team were the Wright brothers—center fielder Harry, the first professional baseball player, and George, a shortstop. George earned $1400—tops on the team. That first season he batted .518, drove in 339 runs and hit 54 home runs. The Red Stockings won all 69 of the games they played that first season and extended their streak to 92 the next year before the Brooklyn Atlantics broke it.

March 15, 1966—The man who was the founder of the Harlem Globetrotters, Abe Saperstein, died.

March 15, 1978—Vida Blue was acquired from Oakland by the San Francisco Giants. The A's received Gary Alexander, Dave Heaverlo, Phillip Huffman, John Johnson, Gary Thomasson, Alan Wirth, Mario Guerrero and cash.

March 15, 1980—Two veteran National Football League quarterbacks changed teams. The Oakland Raiders obtained Dan Pastorini from Houston and the Oilers sent southpaw Ken Stabler to the Raiders.

March 15, 1980—The new ownership of the New York Mets signed pitcher Craig Swan to a five-year, $3-million contract. It was a record for the team and exceeded the $2.1-million contract over a five-year period signed by Lee Mazzilli.

March 16, 1967—In a spring training game—one of the wildest ever—the Red Sox outlasted the New York Mets, 23–18. Boston scored ten times in the ninth inning. Forty hits were made by the two teams in the game that lasted almost four hours.

March 17, 1897—The first boxing match ever filmed took place at Carson City, Nevada. Englishman Bob Fitzsimmons kayoed Jim Corbett in the 14th round to win the heavyweight championship of the world.

March 17, 1902—Bobby Jones, who twenty-eight years later would become the first golfer to win the Grand Slam, was born.

March 17, 1914—Sammy Baugh was born. In 1937, he came out of Texas Christian University to join the Washington Redskins after having tossed a record 599 passes in three seasons. Baugh remained with Washington until 1952. Six times he led the National Football League in passing; six times he was chosen All-Pro.

March 17, 1955—The suspension of Montreal star Maurice Richard and the cancellation of a game between the Canadiens and Detroit after one period with the Red Wings being awarded a 4–1 victory triggered riots and looting that lasted in Montreal for hours.

March 17, 1965—Amos Alonzo Stagg, a football legend, died. He was 102 years old.

March 18, 1953—The National League approved the shifting of the Boston Braves franchise to Milwaukee. Boston was left without major league baseball for the first time since 1876—breaking the pattern of the same sixteen major league teams that had existed since 1903.

March 18, 1959—Bill Sharman of the Boston Celtics sank the first of a record string of fifty-six straight free throws.

March 19, 1954—The first United States boxing match televised in color took place at Madison Square Garden in New York City. Joey Giardello opposed Willy Troy.

March 20, 1897—Yale defeated Penn, 32–10, in what is alleged to be the first collegiate basketball game that featured five players on each team.

March 20, 1948—Hockey great Bobby Orr was born.

March 20, 1973—Pittsburgh Pirate great Roberto Clemente was admitted to baseball's Hall of

Fame. Eleven weeks before, Clemente had died in a plane crash. His tragic death created a condition in which the customary five-year waiting period after a player retires was waived and he was admitted posthumously to the Hall of Fame.

March 21, 1946—Complemented by many former major league players, the Mexican League baseball season began.

March 22, 1894—The first Stanley Cup game in history was played. Montreal defeated Ottawa, 3–1, at Victoria Rink in Montreal, Canada.

March 22, 1904—A patent was issued for an invention called the "Baseball Catcher." It was a box of wood and wire designed to reach from the player's chin to his waist, tied on, with a screen on top to protect the face. The box had two wire doors, hinged to swing inward if struck by a ball. It was a primitive catcher's glove.

March 22, 1967—Muhammad Ali was stripped of his heavyweight title for refusing to be inducted into the United States Army.

March 22, 1969—UCLA trimmed Purdue, 92–72, to become the first college team to win three straight NCAA titles.

March 22, 1974—Peter Revson died. He was one of the top road-racing car drivers in the United States. The cause of his death was a crash during a practice run for the South Africa Grand Prix.

March 23, 1963—John Pennel claimed a new world's record by vaulting sixteen feet, three inches in a Memphis, Tennessee outdoor meet.

March 24, 1893—George Sisler was born in Manchester, Ohio. Twenty-two years later he began a spectacular career as one of baseball's all-time top first basemen.

March 24 and March 25, 1936—The longest game in National Hockey League Stanley Cup history was played. Detroit Red Winger Mud Bruneteau took a pass from Hec Kilrea and scored for a 1–0 victory over the Montreal Maroons. The total playing time for the game was 176 minutes and 30 seconds. The game began at 8:34 P.M. on March 24. Its conclusion came at 2:25 A.M., March 25—five hours and 51 minutes after it began. Detroit goalie Hooley Smith had ninety saves.

March 24, 1962—Emile Griffith battered Benny ("the Kid") Paret into unconsciousness and he had to be carried out of the ring. Ten days later, Paret died.

March 24, 1971—The name of the National Football League's Boston Patriots was changed to the New England Patriots.

March 24, 1973—Three-time National doubles tennis champion Peck Griffin died.

March 25, 1958—Sugar Ray Robinson regained the middleweight boxing championship for the fourth time. The stylish fighter defeated Carmen Basilio in a title fight in Chicago.

March 26, 1926—Georges Vezina, a top goalie for the Montreal Canadiens in 1917–1926, died. The National Hockey League's award for the top goalkeeper each season is named in Vezina's honor.

March 26, 1972—UCLA won its sixth consecutive NCAA basketball championship.

March 26, 1973—George Sisler died in St. Louis, Missouri. Admitted to the Hall of Fame in 1939, Sisler had a lifetime batting average of .340 and twice batted over .400.

March 27, 1972—Adolph Rupp, head basketball coach at the University of Kentucky for forty-two years, retired.

March 28, 1907—Boston Red Sox manager Chick Stahl died in West Baden Springs, Indiana. He had taken poison.

March 28, 1947—Just a year after being inducted into the Hall of Fame, Johnny Evers, who played in the majors for eighteen years, died in Albany, New York.

March 28, 1950—City College of New York became the first basketball team to win both the NCAA championship and the NIT title in the same year.

March 28, 1953—Jim Thorpe died. One of the greatest all-around athletes in American history, he starred in many sports. In the 1912 Olympics, he proved to be the finest all-around track and field man in the world. He won both the decathlon and pentathlon with record-breaking performances. He played major league baseball for eight years. However, football was where he really prevailed. He could run, pass, punt, block, receive and do just about anything on the gridiron. At the time of his death, he was a penniless alcoholic.

March 28, 1963—The New York Titans of the American Football League changed their name to the New York Jets.

March 29, 1867—Cy Young, who would become the only pitcher to win 200 games in each league, was born.

March 30, 1980—Secretariat was foaled. Three years later the famed horse would win the 1973 Triple Crown.

March 31, 1971—Knute Rockne, one of the greatest coaches in collegiate history, was killed in a plane crash.

March 21, 1973—Ken Norton broke Muhammad Ali's jaw and went on to win a split decision in their heavyweight fight.

March 31, 1980—Jesse Owens died of lung cancer at the age of 66 in Tuscon, Arizona. Winner of four gold medals at the Berlin Olympics in 1936, Owens was one of the great track and field athletes in American history. His Olympic triumphs were made even more dramatic and significant because of the political situation that prevailed. Adolph Hitler had viewed the competition as a showcase for Nazi supremacy. The German leader was so angered by the triumphs of Owens, that he refused to shake hands with the black American athlete.

APRIL

April 1, 1930—As an April Fool's Day stunt, Chicago Cub catcher Gabby Hartnett caught baseballs dropped from the Goodyear blimp.

April 2, 1908—Luke Appling was born. Dubbed "Old Aches and Pains," Appling always complained about the real and imagined ailments picked up through 2,422 major league games. At age 43, he was still playing ball. In 1964, his longevity and .310 batting average were a couple of the reasons for his admission to the Hall of Fame.

April 2, 1969—Lew Alcindor (Kareem Abdul-Jabbar) signed a five-year contract with the Milwaukee Bucks of the National Basketball Association and began his illustrious professional career.

April 2, 1972—New York Mets manager Gil Hodges died. He had played eighteen holes of golf and walking back to his West Palm Beach motel room, he collapsed. "He landed on the back of his head," recalls Joe Pignatano who was with the former Brooklyn Dodger star. "He was dead before he hit the ground."

April 3, 1962—One of the all-time great jockeys, Eddie Arcaro, retired.

April 4, 1888—Tris Speaker was born in Hubbard, Texas. Nineteen years later he would appear in a Boston Red Sox uniform. A lifetime .344 hitter, Speaker rapped more doubles (793) than any other player in the history of baseball. In 1928, he concluded his twenty-two-year playing career, and in 1937, was admitted to baseball's Hall of Fame.

April 4, 1924—Gil Hodges was born in Princeton, Indiana. In 1943, he began his career with the Brooklyn Dodgers as one of baseball's steadiest and most popular players. A powerful, right-handed batter, Hodges recorded one hundred or more RBI's a season and more than thirty-two home runs in the years 1949–1955.

April 5, 1913—With regularly scheduled games and leagues existing all over the United States, a need for a national organization for soccer was clear. That need created the United States Soccer Federation. Its creation aided in the work of organizing and unifying soccer, certifying players and providing an international linkage for the sport. The USSF became the sole voice for amateur and professional soccer and the legal guardian of all aspects of the sport in the United States. No U.S. player was able to compete internationally unless that player was a member of an United States Soccer Federation club or league.

April 5, 1965—The color of National Football League penalty flags used by officials was changed from white to bright gold.

April 6, 1903—Mickey Cochrane was born in Bridgewater, Massachusetts. A catcher for thirteen years with the Philadelphia Athletics and Detroit Tigers, he was admitted to baseball's Hall of Fame in 1947.

April 7, 1872—Jersey Joe Walcott, the first black welterweight champion, was born.

April 7, 1963—A 23-year-old Jack Nicklaus won the Masters Golf Tournament.

April 7, 1966—Joe Foss resigned after six years as American Football League commissioner.

April 7, 1979—Ken Forsch pitched a no-hitter against the Atlanta Braves. It was one year and nine days after his brother Bob hurled a no-hitter against Philadelphia, making the Forsch brothers the first pitching brothers to hurl no-hitters.

April 8, 1940—John Havlicek was born. He would grow up to become a star performer for the Boston Celtics and one of the top all-time players in the National Basketball Association. He would also share with Dolph Schayes the record (sixteen years) for the most NBA playing seasons.

April 8, 1946—James Augustus Hunter was born in Hertford, North Carolina. He earned the nickname "Catfish" when he was a small boy because he ran away from home and returned with two catfish. Hunter starred for the Oakland Athletics and New York Yankees and pitched in six

World Series during a fifteen-year major league career.

April 8, 1966—Al Davis, general manager and coach of the Oakland Raiders, was named American Football League commissioner.

April 8, 1969—The first professional baseball game was played at San Diego Stadium. The Padres eked out a 2–1 victory over Houston.

April 8, 1969—Baseball's first international match took place at Shea Stadium in New York City. The Montreal Expos played against the Mets.

April 8, 1978—Ford C. Frick died. Admitted to baseball's Hall of Fame in 1970, he was commissioner of baseball from 1951 to 1965.

April 9, 1912—The Boston Red Sox defeated Harvard University in an exhibition game played during a snowstorm. It was the first game ever played at Fenway Park.

April 9, 1913—The day was cold and windy in Brooklyn, New York. About 12,000 paying customers entered through the grand and ornate rotunda to get through the turnstiles to watch the first regular season game ever played at Ebbets Field. Built at a cost of $750,000, the park's name came from Charles H. Ebbets, who rose from his job selling peanuts and scorecards to become president and principal owner of the Brooklyn Dodgers. The home team lost that day, 1–0, to the Philadelphia Phillies. A Dodger outfielder named Casey Stengel made a sensational catch.

April 9, 1945—Wearing of socks in league games was made mandatory by the NFL.

April 10, 1896—The "Marathon" race was run as part of the Olympics held in Athens, Greece. The distance was about forty kilometers.

April 10, 1971—The first baseball game at Veterans Stadium in Philadelphia took place. The Phillies defeated Montreal, 4–1. The game attendance of 55,352 was the largest at that point in the history of Pennsylvania baseball.

April 10, 1973—Kansas City defeated Texas, 12–1, in the first game ever played at Royals Stadium.

April 11, 1921—The first radio broadcast of a prize fight took place at the Pittsburgh Motor Garden. Johnny Ray defeated Johnny Dundee in ten rounds in a featherweight match.

April 11, 1947—Jackie Robinson became the first black player to wear a major league uniform as he appeared for the Dodgers in an exhibition game against the New York Yankees.

April 11, 1961—Don Drysdale of Los Angeles pitched his fourth straight opening day game for the Dodgers.

April 11, 1966—Jack Nicklaus scored his second straight and third Masters golf tournament win.

April 12, 1877—The catcher's mask was used for the first time in a baseball game. The pioneer was James Alexander Tyng who wore the mask in a game played at Lynn, Massachusetts.

April 12, 1977—Phil K. Wrigley, the owner of the Chicago Cubs since 1932, died. The park the team plays in was named for him.

April 13, 1972—A thirteen-day player strike, the first engaged in by major league baseball in history, ended.

April 14, 1942—Pete Rose was born in Cincinnati, Ohio. He would star as a hometown player for the Reds for sixteen years and then sign a multi-million dollar contract to play for the Philadelphia Phillies.

April 14, 1960—Philadelphia Phillies manager Eddie Sawyer resigned. An opening day loss on April 12th was given as one of the reasons Sawyer cleared out. Gene Mauch was promoted from Minneapolis to become the new Philadelphia manager.

April 14, 1969—Canada's first major league baseball game took place at Montreal's tiny Jarry Park. More than a thousand fans jammed into the park beyond the official seating capacity. The Expos delighted their fans with an 8–7 triumph over the defending National League champions —the St. Louis Cardinals.

April 15, 1915—In 1908 Jack Johnson became the first black heavyweight champion of the world.

He was a little over six feet tall, a little over 200 pounds, and a little too flashy for his times. He wore mod clothes and drove yellow racing cars at reckless speeds. He was also continually in trouble because of public brawling. There was also a great deal of prejudice against Johnson because he was a black and a search for "the great white hope" began almost the instant he won the heavyweight championship. Jim Jeffries was talked out of a six-year retirement and put in the ring against Johnson. It took the efforts of gigantic Jess Willard through twenty-six rounds in the heat of Havana to finally strip the title away from Johnson. But the fight on that April 15, 1915, still remains as one of the most controversial moments in sports history. Many maintain that Johnson threw the fight in order to please federal authorities so that he might be permitted to return to the United States. Johnson was accused of violating the Mann Act by abducting a nineteen-year-old white girl across statelines for immoral purposes. The charges were false. The girl was a known prostitute; however, Johnson claimed that he was offered a deal—lose the championship and get permission to have the charges dropped and return to the United States. The fight ended with Johnson being counted out—lying on his back—his arms covering his face—some say out of shame.

April 15, 1947—Jackie Robinson, grandson of slaves, broke baseball's color line by playing first base for the Brooklyn Dodgers at Ebbets Field. Many of the fans wore "I'm for Jackie" buttons and cheered the debut of the 28-year-old Robinson.

April 15, 1954—The Baltimore Orioles played the first game in Memorial Stadium defeating the Chicago White Sox, 3–1.

April 15, 1978—Joe "Flash" Gordon died. He was a second baseman for the New York Yankees and Cleveland Indians from 1938 to 1950.

April 15, 1980—The largest crowd in National Basketball Association history, 40,172, saw the Milwaukee Bucks defeat the Seattle Supersonics at the Kingdome. The victory gave the Bucks a 3–2 lead in their NBA playoff round with the Sonics.

April 16, 1929—The New York Yankees appeared with numbers on their uniforms—thus becoming the first team to do so on a permanent basis.

April 16, 1940—Cleveland's Bob Feller pitched the only no-hit, no-run opening day game in baseball history.

April 16, 1947—Lew Alcindor, who would later change his name to Kareem Abdul-Jabbar, was born in New York City. The only child of a 6'-2" New York transit policeman and a 6' housewife, he was 22½ inches long at birth and weighed twelve pounds, eleven ounces. At thirteen, Kareem was 6'-8" and 200 pounds and rounding into the form that would enable him to score more points and record more rebounds than any other player in New York City high school basketball history.

April 17, 1820—Alexander Cartwright, the man who designed the baseball diamond, was born.

April 17, 1963—For allegedly gambling on NFL games, Paul Hornung of Green Bay and Alex Karras of Detroit, were suspended by Commissioner Pete Rozelle.

April 17, 1964—The first game ever played at Shea Stadium took place. Pittsburgh defeated the New York Mets, 4–3. Willie Stargell's second inning home run was the first hit in the new ballpark. The first Met hit was recorded by Tim Harkness in the third inning.

April 18, 1923—Yankee Stadium was officially opened. The National Anthem was played by John Philip Sousa's band. Governor Al Smith threw out the first ball and Babe Ruth hit a home run. A crowd of 74,000 attended, a record unbroken for thirty-one years.

April 18, 1956—Officiating a game between the New York Yankees and the Washington Senators, Ed Rommel became the first umpire to wear glasses while on duty.

April 18, 1966—Bill Russell became the player-coach of the Boston Celtics.

April 18, 1966—The first annual United States marathon was staged. It stretched 26 miles, 385 feet from Hopkinton, Mass. to Boston.

April 19, 1900—The highest scoring opening day game in National League history took place.

The Phillies defeated Boston, 19–17, in 10 innings. Boston had scored nine runs in the ninth inning to send the game into extra innings.

April 19, 1958—The Los Angeles Dodgers faced the San Francisco Giants in a baseball game at the Los Angeles Coliseum—and with the two teams opposing each other for the first time in California—major league ball became a permanent fixture on the West Coast.

April 19, 1966—The first major league game ever played at Anaheim Stadium took place. Almost 32,000 came out to see California play the Chicago White Sox.

April 20, 1939—Ted Williams recorded the first of his 2,654 major league hits. It was a double off Yankee pitcher Red Ruffing that rocketed off the 407-foot sign in Yankee Stadium's right center field.

April 20, 1949—Jockey Willie Shoemaker won his first race aboard Shafter at Golden Gate Fields in Albany, California.

April 21, 1925—More than 100,000 lined the procession route for the funeral of Charles H. Ebbets, who rose from peanut seller to president of the Brooklyn baseball club and had the team's ballpark named for him.

April 21, 1944—The National Football League mandated that the Chicago Cardinals and Pittsburgh Steelers merge for one year under the

name Card-Pitt. The new team name was pro-
nounced "carpet." The team's record under-
scored its name, for every team in the league
walked over it. The "Carpets" ended their one-
year experimental merger with a record of no
wins and ten losses.

April 21, 1972—Texas edged California, 7–6, in
the first major league baseball game ever played
at Arlington Stadium.

April 21, 1980—Bill Rodgers won his third
straight Boston Marathon—his time was two
hours, twelve minutes and eleven seconds.

April 22, 1876—Boston trimmed Philadelphia,
6–5, in the first official game in National League
history. The other charter clubs in that eight-
team league were: Chicago, New York, Hartford,
St. Louis, Cincinnati and Louisville. Admission
fees for games were seventy-five cents with a bar-
gain rate of ten cents in operation after the third
inning.

April 22, 1915—Pinstripes appeared for the first
time on the uniforms of the New York Yankees.

April 22, 1962—The Toronto Maple Leafs, for
the first time since 1951, won the National Hockey League Stanley Cup.

April 23, 1921—Warren Spahn was born in Buffalo, New York. He would pitch twenty-one years
in the major leagues, win nearly 400 games and
be admitted to the Hall of Fame in 1973.

April 23, 1964—The first no-hit loss in baseball history was recorded by Ken Johnson. The Houston pitcher lost 1–0 to Cincinnati who capitalized on two errors made by Johnson's teammates.

April 24, 1909—"Home Run" Baker recorded his only grand slam home run.

April 24, 1951—The Soviet Union applied for Olympic competition. Up to this point in time Russia had never competed in the Olympics.

April 24, 1963—Bob Cousy of the Boston Celtics, one of pro basketball's greatest players, retired.

April 25, 1873—At Creedmoor, Long Island in New York State, the first shooting meet of the National Rifle Association took place.

April 25, 1950—The Boston Celtics selected Chuck Cooper in the National Basketball Association draft and broke the league's color line. Cooper, who was an all-America forward at Duquesne, was the first black chosen to play in the NBA. Cooper was selected in the second round of the draft by the Celtics; Earl Lloyd, another black player, was picked in the ninth round of the draft by the Washington Capitols. Lloyd actually played in an NBA game twenty-four hours earlier than Cooper and was thus the first black to ever appear in a league game.

April 26, 1917—Sal Maglie was born. He would be dubbed "the Barber" because of his style of pitching that "shaved" batters close. He would be one of the few pitchers in history to perform for three New York City baseball teams—the Dodgers, the Giants and the Yankees.

April 26, 1952—Paddy Berg carded an 18-hole, 64, a women's record for a major golf tourney.

April 27, 1938—The first use of a yellow baseball took place in a Columbia-Fordham baseball game.

April 27, 1947—Baseball Commissioner "Happy" Chandler designated this date as "Babe Ruth Day" to honor the Yankee great. Simultaneous ceremonies took place before each major league game played that day. Stooped, shrunken, a shell of his once-powerful self, the Babe appeared at Yankee Stadium, ravaged by throat cancer. His topcoat seemed two sizes too large as he said good-bye to the 70,000-plus fans who came to honor him.

April 27, 1956—Rocky Marciano retired from professional boxing. Winner of all of his forty-nine pro fights, all but six by knockouts, Marciano joined Gene Tunney as only the second heavyweight champ to retire undefeated.

April 27, 1961—Canton, Ohio, where the NFL was formed in 1920, was chosen as the site of the Professional Football Hall of Fame.

April 28, 1946—The Boston Red Sox moved into first place and stayed there for the rest of the season.

April 28, 1961—In Milwaukee, just five after his fortieth birthday, Warren Spahn pitched the second no-hitter of his long career.

April 28, 1974—Before 53,775 fans in Atlanta Stadium and millions more who watched on national television, Hank Aaron blasted a fourth inning pitch over the left centerfield fence. It was home run number 715 of his career and broke Babe Ruth's historic record. The pitch was thrown by Al Downing, who wore the same uniform number as Aaron, 44. The home run ball was caught by relief pitcher Tom House in the Atlanta bullpen.

April 29, 1941—The Bees baseball team of Boston had their name changed to Braves.

April 29, 1947—Jim Ryun, one of the great figures in United States track history, was born. In 1966, he would be rated as the world's greatest athlete.

April 30, 1946—Don Schollander was born. He would become the first swimmer to win four gold medals in one Olympic (1964).

MAY

May 1, 1920—In Boston, the starting pitchers were Leon Cadore for the Brooklyn Dodgers and Joe Oeschger for the Braves. Both pitchers yielded one run; both pitchers hurled twenty-six innings. The game was called because of darkness. It was the longest major league game ever played. "I found myself growing sleepy at the finish," Cadore joked.

May 1, 1920—Babe Ruth slammed his first home run as a member of the Yankees. Herb Pennock tossed the home run pitch.

May 1, 1923—Earl Sande, an all-time great jockey, won his first Kentucky Derby aboard Zev.

May 1, 1946—Catcher Clyde Klutz in the space of four hours was a member of three different major league teams. In St. Louis with the New York Giants, Klutz was told at 9:00 a.m. that he had been traded to the Philadelphia Phillies for Vince DiMaggio. "Stay close to the hotel," Giant manager Mel Ott said, "you'll be hearing from the Phillies in a couple of hours." Klutz did not hear from the Phillies about his next move. He heard from Cardinal manager Eddie Dyer who told him that he had been obtained by St. Louis for Emil Verban. It proved a lucky day for Klutz. As a member of the Cardinals, who won the first playoff in National League history and the 1946 World Series, he was able to pocket almost $4,000 as a winner's share.

May 1, 1948—Eddie Arcaro rode Citation to victory in the Kentucky Derby. Arcaro became the first jockey to win four derbies. The six-horse field was the smallest since 1907.

May 1, 1954—Stan Musial of the St. Louis Cardinals hammered a record five home runs in a doubleheader against the New York Giants.

May 1, 1955—Cleveland's Bob Feller hurled his twelfth and final one-hitter in a 2–0 victory over Baltimore.

May 2, 1917—Baseball's first double no-hit game took place at Wrigley Field in Chicago. Both Hippo Vaughn of the Cubs and Cincinnati's Fred Toney pitched no-hit ball for nine innings. Cincinnati won the game, 1–0, in the tenth.

May 2, 1939—A baseball record that will probably never be broken ended. Lou Gehrig, after playing 2,130 consecutive games for the New York Yankees, benched himself in a game against Detroit.

May 2, 1953—A 25–1 underdog, Dark Star, nosed out the favored Native Dancer and won the Kentucky Derby.

May 3, 1920—Walker Smith was born. He would be better known as Sugar Ray Robinson, one of the greatest boxers in history and the only man to win a world title five times.

May 3, 1941—Eddie Arcaro rode Whirlaway to victory in the Kentucky Derby.

May 3, 1952—A fifth Kentucky Derby win was recorded by Eddie Arcaro. The illustrious jockey rode Hill Gail to victory.

May 3, 1980—A filly won the Kentucky Derby for the first time in sixty-five years. Genuine Risk came out of the pack at the head of the stretch and moved in front of a dozen struggling males to win the race by a length. The last filly to enter the Kentucky Derby was Silver Spoon in 1959. The last filly to win the Derby was Regret in 1915.

May 4, 1940—In one of the biggest upsets in Kentucky Derby history, Gallahadion defeated Bimelech. The winning purse of $60,150 was a record to that point in time.

May 5, 1849—Hambletonian was foaled by a crippled mare under a bunch of oak trees on a New York farm. Dubbed the Father of the Breed, between 1851–1874, Hambletonian sired 1,331 foals.

May 5, 1973—Secretariat won the Kentucky Derby in the record time of 1:59.2.

May 6, 1915—Yankee pitcher Jack Warhop tossed the pitch that Babe Ruth hit for his first major league home run. The historic homer was recorded at Yankee Stadium.

May 6, 1931—Willie Mays was born in Westfield, Alabama. Twenty years later he joined the New York Giants and began his illustrious twenty-two year major league baseball career.

May 6, 1954—Roger Bannister became the first person in history to run a mile in under four minutes. In a race at Oxford, England, Bannister ran the mile in 3:59.4.

May 7, 1925—Glenn Wright of the Pittsburgh Pirates became the fifth man in major league baseball history to perform an unassisted triple play.

May 7, 1933—Johnny Unitas was born. He would go straight from high school into professional football and become one of the great quarterbacks in the history of the sport.

May 7, 1959—The largest crowd in baseball history—93,103—watched an exhibition game between the New York Yankees and the Los Angeles Dodgers at the Coliseum in Los Angeles. It was "Roy Campanella Night" and the former Brooklyn Dodger catcher was pushed in a wheelchair onto the playing field by his former teammate, Pee Wee Reese. On January 28, 1958, Campanella was paralyzed as a result of an automobile accident. "I want to thank God," Campy told all those in attendance, "that I'm here alive and able to see this. I want to thank each and every one of you from the bottom of my heart. This is something I'll never forget." The irony of "Roy Campanella Night" was that it was a tribute by the people of Los Angeles for a player they had never seen perform on California soil.

May 8, 1954—Parry O'Brien threw the shot put 60 feet, 5¼ inches to become the first performer ever to exceed 60 feet in the event.

May 8, 1961—They could have been the New York Continentals or Burros or Skyliners or Skyscrapers or Bees or Rebels or NYB's or Avengers or even Jets (all runner-up names in the contest to tab the National League team that represented New York and began playing ball in 1962.) On this date, the name chosen for the team was The New York Mets.

May 9, 1870—Golfer Harry Vardon was born. The award for the performer with the lowest average each year on the pro tour is named for Vardon, a six-time British Open winner.

May 10, 1910—Jimmy Demaret was born. He would become the first golfer to win three Masters tournaments.

May 10, 1913—A 91-1 long shot, Donerail stunned the racing world by winning the Kentucky Derby.

May 10, 1947—Famed announcer Clem McCarthy created the biggest blunder of his career. He told a national radio audience listening to his description of the 1947 Preakness Stakes horse race that Faultless was the winner of the race. Jet Pilot was actually the winner.

May 10, 1969—A merger of the National Football League and the American Football League was announced for the 1970–1971 season.

May 10, 1970—Nearly 47-years-old, Hoyt Wilhelm of the Atlanta Braves made his 1,000th pitching appearance—a ninth inning relief job against the St. Louis Cardinals.

May 11, 1946—The first night game ever played in Boston took place at Braves Field. It was a game in which Hall of Famer Paul Waner recorded his 3,000th hit.

May 11, 1972—Willie Mays was traded by the San Francisco Giants to the New York Mets.

May 12, 1917—Omar Khayyam became the first imported horse to record a Kentucky Derby victory.

May 12, 1925—Lawrence Peter Berra, destined to be known as "Yogi" and become one of the great catchers in baseball history, was born in St. Louis, Missouri.

May 13, 1978—Joie Ray died. In 1924, this track star set the record of four minutes and twelve seconds for the world's indoor mile.

May 13, 1980—For the first time in his career, Fred Lynn of the Boston Red Sox hit for the cycle to lead his teammates to a 10–5 triumph over the Twins.

May 14, 1874—Admission fees were charged and goal posts were used for the first time in a football game as McGill played Harvard at Cambridge, Massachusetts.

May 14, 1904—St. Louis, Missouri was the site of the start of the first Olympic Games held in the United States.

May 14, 1967—Mickey Mantle hit his 500th home run.

May 14, 1968—Don Drysdale of the Dodgers began a string of pitching 58 2/3 innings of scoreless innings that eventually wiped out Walter Johnson's all-time record of 56 straight scoreless innings set in 1913.

May 15, 1862—Baseball's first enclosed park—Brooklyn's Union Grounds—opened.

May 15, 1926—An ice hockey franchise was granted to the New York Rangers.

May 15, 1941—Joe DiMaggio's record 56-game hitting streak began.

May 15, 1953—Rocky Marciano jolted Jersey Joe Walcott by knocking him out in two minutes and twenty-five seconds in their heavyweight bout in Chicago.

May 16, 1928—Billy Martin was born in Berkeley, California. Twenty-two years later he would become a member of the New York Yankees. Fifty-two years later he would return to California to manage the Oakland Athletics.

May 16, 1939—The first night game in the American League took place. Cleveland opposed the Athletics at Philadelphia's Shibe Park.

May 17, 1875—The first Kentucky Derby was run. Aristides was the winner.

May 17, 1939—A Princeton-Columbia baseball game at Baker Field in New York City provided the subject matter for the first televised sporting event in history. The transmission was over station W2XBS by a sixteen-man NBC crew using equipment that cost $100,000. A single camera was used, and the total cost of transmittal was $3,000. There were no close-ups of action. The players on the television screen looked like white flies. The single camera was stationed near the third base line, and it swept back and forth across the diamond. Monday Night Football, the Super Bowl and the World Series at night in prime time were in the future, but their roots can be traced to that spring day in 1939.

May 17, 1970—Hank Aaron became the ninth player in major league history to record his 3,000th hit.

May 17, 1979—The Philadelphia Phillies edged the Chicago Cubs, 23–22, in one of the highest scoring games ever played. Eleven home runs were hit by the two teams to tie a major league record.

May 18, 1942—All night baseball games in New York City were banned until the conclusion of World War II. It was felt that the glow from the lights in the ball parks would present a danger to shipping vessels.

May 18, 1946—Reggie Jackson was born in Wyncote, Pennsylvania. Twenty-one years later he made his major league baseball debut as a rookie outfielder with the Kansas City Athletics.

May 19, 1928—Dolph Schayes was born. He would be a twelve-time National Basketball Association all-star.

May 19, 1956—Dale Long of the Pittsburgh Pirates began a record streak during which he hit eight home runs. The streak ended on May 28th.

May 19, 1961—Jockey Willie Shoemaker won his 4,000th race.

May 20, 1939—Joe Carr, Commissioner of the National Football League since 1921, died.

May 20, 1964—Pitcher Don Larsen was sold to Houston by the San Francisco Giants.

May 21, 1904—Representatives of Belgium, Denmark, France, Holland, Spain, Sweden and Switzerland met in Paris and formed the Federation Internationale de Football—the world ruling body of soccer.

May 21, 1980—Paul Silas signed a three-year contract to become the player-coach of the San Diego Clippers in the National Basketball Association. Silas, a 36-year-old grandfather, began his pro career with the St. Louis Hawks in the 1964–1965 season. Only John Havlicek of the Boston Celtics played in more games than Silas, 1,270 to 1,254 for Silas. "I would like to have the record," Silas said at the time of his signing, "for it's important to me . . . but not so important that I would let it mess up my new team."

May 22, 1943—Tommy John was born in Terre Haute, Indiana. Twenty years later he appeared as a pitcher for the Cleveland Indians and began his career as one of the top hurlers in major league baseball.

May 22, 1958—Joe Louis was ordered by the United States Court of Appeals in Chicago to turn over the trust funds he created in the 1940's for his children. The court order wanted the trust fund as payment for the legendary heavyweight champion's tax bills.

May 22, 1975—Lefty Grove died. A Hall of Fame pitcher, he won 300 games as a member of the Boston Red Sox and Philadelphia Athletics.

May 23, 1876—Joe Borden of Boston pitched baseball's first no-hitter.

May 23, 1922—Gene Tunney suffered the first and only loss in his boxing career. Harry Greb was the winner in a decision in their fifteen round light heavyweight championship bout.

May 23, 1941—Joe Louis defeated Buddy Baer to record his seventeenth successful defense of his heavyweight championship.

May 23, 1962—The Philadelphia Warriors moved their National Basketball Association franchise to San Francisco.

May 24, 1935—Baseball's first night game was played at Crosley Field in Cincinnati. The Reds defeated the Phillies, 2–1.

May 24, 1950—Sold by the Harlem Globetrotters to the New York Knickerbockers, Nat "Sweetwater" Clifton became the third black player in the National Basketball Association.

May 24, 1967—Cincinnati became the tenth franchise in the American Football League. Paul Brown functioned as head coach, general-manager and part-owner of the team.

May 24, 1980—The New York Islanders scored a 5–4 overtime victory over the Philadelphia Flyers to win the Stanley Cup. Bob Nystrom's goal at seven minutes and eleven seconds of the sudden-death overtime was his second of the game and thrilled the thousands of fans at the Nassau Coliseum in Uniondale, Long Island. It was a dramatic victory for the Islander franchise, which was just eight years old. The Stanley Cup triumph was the first for a New York City area team since the Rangers won in 1940; it was only the second Stanley Cup win for a National Hockey League expansion team. Ironically, that team was the Flyers of 1974 and 1975 whom the Islanders defeated. The Islander victory ended the National Hockey League season that began in October of 1979. Bryan Trottier of the Islanders was voted the Conn Smythe Trophy as the most valuable player in the playoffs. Trottier had two assists in the game and broke the record for most playoff points with 29. Bob Nystrom, whose goal clinched the first Stanley Cup victory for the Islanders said: "The guys on this team weren't willing to die. That label that we were losers, we'd heard enough of that. We're winners." An interesting note to the Islander victory was Ken Morrow, who became the first player to be on the United States gold medal Olympic ice hockey team and a Stanley Cup champion.

May 25, 1898—Gene Tunney was born. He would be the heavyweight champion of the world from 1926 to 1928. Winner of 56 out of his 57 fights—41 of them by knockouts—Tunney twice defeated Jack Dempsey.

May 25, 1926—Bill Sharman was born. He would star for the Boston Celtics in the N.B.A. for a decade. A slick-shooting guard, Sharman was one of the most accurate free throw shooters in professional basketball history.

May 25, 1935—Babe Ruth had his last hurrah. Performing as a part-time player and assistant manager for the Boston Braves, Ruth blasted three home runs in a game in Pittsburgh. His last home run—the final shot of his career—was a towering drive over the right field roof. No one had ever hit a home run that cleared that roof and it was fitting that Ruth's final homer— number 714—was the one that did it.

May 25, 1951—The New York Giants called up a twenty-year-old named Willie Howard Mays. The youngster was hitting .477 for the Minneapolis farm team of the Giants.

May 25, 1973—An American women's javelin mark of 207 feet, 10 inches was set by Kathy Schmidt in the California Relays in Modesto.

May 25, 1980—Johnny Rutherford won the Indianapolis 500 for the third time in seven years. He also became the first driver in the sixty-four years of the competition to win the event twice from the pole position.

May 25, 1980—Polish athlete Wszola, the 1976 Olympic high-jump champion, set a world record in the high-jump clearing 7'8½" at Heilbronn, West Germany. It was the first time since 1912 that an American or Soviet performer did not hold the high-jump record.

May 26, 1959—Harvey Haddix of the Pittsburgh Pirates pitched a perfect game for twelve innings and lost the perfect game and the no-hitter in the thirteenth inning when Hank Aaron homered for a 1–0 Milwaukee Brave victory.

May 26, 1980—It was a good day for the St. Louis Cardinals and for Rick Cerone of the New York Yankees. Cerone pounded his first major league grand-slam home run; the Cardinals defeated the New York Mets, 8–5, and snapped a ten-game losing streak.

May 27, 1873—The first Preakness Stakes was run. Survivor was the winner in the historic race held at Pimlico Race Track in Baltimore, Maryland.

May 27, 1957—Permission was granted by National League owners to the New York Giants and Brooklyn Dodgers to move to California if they so desired.

May 27, 1968—New franchises were awarded to San Diego and Montreal expanding the National League to a dozen teams.

May 28, 1888—Jim Thorpe was born. He would become one of the great athletes in American history.

May 28, 1938—Jerry West was born. His scoring ability would make him one of the top players in the history of the NBA.

May 28, 1946—The first Yankee Stadium night game was played.

May 28, 1953—Edmund Hilary became the first man in history to climb Mt. Everest.

May 28, 1975—Ezzard Charles died. He was the heavyweight boxing champion of the world from 1949 to 1951.

May 29, 1951—Pitcher Billy Joe Davidson was signed to a then record bonus contract of $120,000 by the Cleveland Indians.

May 29, 1962—Buck O'Neil became major league baseball's first black coach when he began work with the Chicago Cubs.

May 29, 1980—By winning his sixth National Basketball Association Most Valuable Player award, Kareem Abdul-Jabbar broke the record of five MVP titles earned by Bill Russell. The Los Angeles Laker star also became the sixteenth straight center to win the award. Abdul-Jabbar in the 1979–80 season was sixth in scoring (24.8) a game, eighth in rebounding (10.8) a game. He paced the league in blocked shots and was second in field-goal percentage. Although a former great Boston Celtic star, Russell had his MVP award record broken by Abdul-Jabbar, the NBA gave major awards for the 1979–80 season to members of the Celtics. Larry Bird won the rookie of the year title; Bill Fitch was selected as coach of the year; Red Auerbach was picked as executive of the year. Bird received 63 of 66 votes; Abdul-Jabbar's teammate, Magic Johnson, received the other three votes for the Rookie of the Year award.

May 30, 1894—A major league baseball player hit four home runs in one game for the first time in history. The player was Bobby Lowe of Boston in a game against Cincinnati.

May 30, 1922—One of baseball's most unusual oddities took place during a morning-afternoon doubleheader in Chicago. Max Flack played right field for the Cubs in the first game. Cliff Heathcote played right field for the Cardinals. There was a two-hour wait between games during which Flack was traded for Heathcote. In the second game, Heathcote took Flack's position in right field for the Cubs; Flack assumed Heathcote's old job for the Cardinals.

May 30, 1927—Jimmy Cooney of the Chicago Cubs became the sixth player in major league history to notch an unassisted triple play.

May 30, 1937—Carl Hubbell pitched his 24th straight victory, a streak of winning games that began in 1936.

May 30, 1943—Gale Sayers, who would star for the Chicago Bears in the National Football League, was born.

May 30, 1976—Max Carey died. He was an outfielder for the Pittsburgh Pirates and the Brooklyn Dodgers. He stole 738 bases during his major league career.

May 31, 1927—Detroit's Johnny Neun became the seventh player in history to execute an unassisted triple play.

May 31, 1938—Henry Armstrong won the world welterweight title defeating Barney Ross.

May 31, 1943—Joe Namath was born. On this date twenty-five years later, the New York Jet quarterback would be selected National Football League Player of the Year.

May 31, 1964—The New York Mets and San Francisco Giants played a 23-inning marathon game that lasted seven hours and twenty-three minutes.

JUNE

June 1, 1925—Lou Gehrig of the New York Yankees played in the first of his record 2,130 straight games, replacing Wally Pipp as the first baseman.

June 1, 1957—At Stockton, California, Don Bowden became the first American to run the mile in less than four minutes—his time—three minutes and 58.7 seconds.

June 1, 1967—The shortest odds ever given were quoted for Dragon Blood (10,000 to 1). Jockey Lester Piggot rode the horse to victory in the Premio Naviglio in Milan, Italy.

June 2, 1941—Lou Gehrig died. He was just seventeen days shy of his 38th birthday.

June 3, 1851—Baseball's first uniformed team made their appearance. The New York Knickerbockers showed up for a game in straw hats, white shirts and blue pants.

June 3, 1888—Baseball's most famous poem, "Casey At The Bat" by Ernest L. Thayer, was published in the *San Francisco Examiner.*

June 3, 1932—Giant manager John J. McGraw retired from baseball because of illness. He had led the Giants to ten pennants and three world championships.

June 3, 1932—Lou Gehrig blasted four home runs in four trips to the plate. He almost managed a fifth straight homer except for an exceptional catch of his long drive by Al Simmons.

June 4, 1953—Ralph Kiner of the Pittsburgh Pirates was the key figure in a ten-player trade between Pittsburgh and the Chicago Cubs. The Pirate slugger was traded by Branch Rickey along with Howie Pollet, Joe Garagiola, and George Metkovitch to the Cubs for Bob Schultz, Toby Atwell, Preston Ward, Gene Freese, Bob Addis and Gene Hermanski. The Cubs sweetened the trade by also shipping $100,000 to the Pirates.

June 4, 1964—Sandy Koufax pitched his third career no-hitter and tied the record set by Cleveland's Bob Feller.

June 4, 1974—Hank Aaron blasted the sixteenth grand-slam home run of his career—a National League record.

June 4, 1980—Gordie Howe announced his retirement from hockey after thirty-two seasons. The 52-year-old Howe, a living legend, left behind momentous achievements: he scored 1,071 goals including a record 801 in the National Hockey League; he tallied 1,518 assists, played in 2,421 games, notched six NHL scoring titles, recorded six Most Valuable Player awards (five of them were won in the NHL for a record)—the other was collected by Howe at the age of 46 when he played in the World Hockey League. "The one record I'm very proud of," said Howe, "is the longevity record." No one ever played more years of professional hockey. Even in his last season, 1979–80, Howe played in all eighty games for the New England Whalers, filling out his career average of sixty-eight games a season.

June 5, 1948—A modern National League rookie record was tied by Richie Ashburn of the Philadelphia Phillies. Ashburn hit safely in his twenty-third straight game to help pace the Phillies to a 6–5 win over the Chicago Cubs.

June 6, 1890—This was the birth date of the United States Polo Association.

June 6, 1907—Bill Dickey was born. He would star as a catcher for the New York Yankees and be admitted to the Hall of Fame in 1954.

June 6, 1946—The National Basketball Association was founded. It was known then as the Basketball Association of America. The BAA had franchises in eleven cities: Boston, New York, Philadelphia, Providence, Toronto, Washington, Chicago, St. Louis, Cleveland, Detroit and Pittsburgh.

June 6, 1967—The National Hockey League expanded by adding six new teams for the 1967–

1968 season—an entire new division. The new teams were: Philadelphia Flyers, Pittsburgh Penguins, Los Angeles Kings, St. Louis Blues, Minnesota North Stars and San Francisco Seals. It was the most ambitious expansion in the history of sports.

June 7, 1892—Baseball's first pinch-hitter, John Joseph Doyle, came to bat for the Cleveland Spiders in a game against the Brooklyn Ward's Wonders.

June 7, 1938—A storied controversy took place at Fenway Park in Boston. Umpire Bill McGowan advised Cleveland Indian pitcher Johnny Allen to cut off part of his sweat shirt sleeve. McGowan maintained that the dangling shirt sleeve distracted batters. Allen was not agreeable. He walked off the mound and refused to return. He was fined $250.00, but his shirt was sent to the Hall of Fame.

June 7, 1947—Thurman Munson was born in Akron, Ohio. Twenty-two years later he would become a member of the New York Yankees.

June 7, 1980—The winner of the 112th running of the Belmont Stakes was Temperence Hill, a 53–1 shot. Genuine Risk, the filly who was the Kentucky Derby winner and finished second in the Preakness, attempted to hold off the stretch drive of the 53–1 shot but could not. Temperence Hill returned $108.80 for a two dollar bet. Eddie Maple, who rode Temperence Hill to victory, recalled the feeling: "I was able to drop in between

Codex and the filly [Genuine Risk]. I figured I was following the right two. Then my horse did everything I asked. I could smell the carnations or whatever they are. This is the greatest day of my life."

June 8, 1950—The "Massacre of Fenway Park" took place. The Red Sox defeated the St. Louis Browns, 29-4. Six club records were set: most runs scored in a game (29); most extra base hits (17); nine doubles, one triple, seven home runs; most extra bases on long hits (32); most runs for two games (49)—the day before the Red Sox had scored twenty runs against the Browns; most hits in two games (51)—the Red Sox collected 23 hits on June 7th and 28 on June 8th.

June 8, 1961—Four Milwaukee Brave batters hit successive home runs in the seventh inning in a game against the Cincinnati Reds.

June 8, 1966—The National Football League and the American Football League agreed to merge into one league of twenty-four teams and to expand to twenty-six teams by 1968. Pete Rozelle was named Commissioner. The league agreed to play separate schedules until 1970 and to meet in a championship game starting in 1967.

June 8, 1968—Don Drysdale's record string of scoreless innings ended at 58 2/3 when a fly ball by Howie Bedell allowed Tony Taylor of the Phillies to tag up and score from third base.

June 8, 1969—After eighteen seasons and twelve World Series, Mickey Mantle of the New York

Yankees retired and concluded one of baseball's most illustrious careers.

June 8, 1980—Ken Boyer was fired as manager of the last place St. Louis Cardinals. The former star third baseman was fired between games of a St. Louis-Montreal Expo doubleheader. His team had lost 19 of its last 23 games and was in last place in the Eastern Division of the National League. It was announced that former Kansas City Royal manager Whitey Herzog would take over as Boyer's successor.

June 9, 1899—Bob Fitzsimmons was one of the most unusual physical specimens to ever perform in a boxing ring. He had a heavyweight's torso, a lightweight's head, and a middleweight's legs. During his career, he was at different times middleweight champ of the world, light-heavyweight champ and heavyweight champ. He did not care about the size or shape or reputation of an opponent. He fought all comers from all over the world. Fitzsimmons had defeated Gentleman Jim Corbett for the heavyweight championship and chose Jim Jeffries as his first opponent as he got ready to defend his crown. The bout took place on this warm June day at the Seaside Sporting Club in Coney Island. Jeffries outweighed Fitzsimmons by about fifty pounds. In the eleventh round, Fitzsimmons went down and out and a new champion was crowned. It was age that had caught up with Fitzsimmons not Jeffries. Bob Fitzsimmons had fought his first bout when Jeffries was five years old.

June 9, 1951—Dave Parker was born in Cincinnati. He would grow up to be 6'5" and 225 pounds and personify the talent on his Pittsburgh Pirates team.

June 9, 1973—In winning the Belmont Stakes, Secretariat became horse racing's first United States triple crown winner in 25 years.

June 10, 1892—Wilbert Robinson of the Baltimore Orioles stroked seven hits in seven times at bat. This hitting record stood until 1975 when Rennie Stennett of Pittsburgh went seven-for-seven against the Chicago Cubs.

June 10, 1975—Pele signed a three-year contract with the Cosmos, just 250 days after retiring from his Santos, Brazil team. His efforts did much to make soccer boom in the United States.

June 11, 1913—Vince Lombardi was born. He would gain fame and fortune with the Green Bay Packers and personify the stereotype of what a football coach was supposed to be like.

June 11, 1938—Johnny Vander Meer hurled a no-hitter against Boston to lead the Reds to an 8–0 victory.

June 11, 1950—Ben Hogan, who survived a severe automobile accident, came back to win the United States Open Championship. Hogan triumphed in a three-way playoff.

June 12, 1880—Baseball's first perfect game was pitched by John Lee Richmond. The Worcester southpaw accomplished the pitching gem against Cleveland. He stood only forty-five feet from home plate and had to throw underhand.

June 12, 1939—Baseball's Hall of Fame was dedicated at Cooperstown, New York. The first memento to be hung in the museum was a pair of shoes with gleaming spikes. "That takes care of Ty Cobb," said the judges.

June 12, 1947—Babe Zaharias became the first American to win the British women's amateur golf tournament.

June 13, 1940—The Chicago Cubs and the Boston Red Sox became the first teams to play at Doubleday Field at Cooperstown, New York.

June 13, 1948—Babe Ruth's uniform was retired and sent to the Hall of Fame.

June 14, 1926—Don Newcombe was born in Madison, New Jersey. He would join the Brooklyn Dodgers in 1949 and become one of baseball's first star black pitchers.

June 14, 1957—The Atlantic Coast Conference was organized.

June 14, 1964—The St. Louis Cardinals made perhaps the best trade in their history sending pitcher Ernie Broglio to the Cubs in return for Lou Brock. One of the greatest of Cardinal players, Brock went on to set the record for the most stolen bases in a season and in a career.

Broglio faded rather quickly from the major
league scene.

June 15, 1909—Patent No. 924,696 was awarded
to Benjamin Shibe for his invention of the cork
center baseball.

June 15, 1938—By pitching the Cincinnati Reds
to a 6–0 win over the Dodgers at Ebbets Field,
Johnny Vander Meer became the first hurler to
record two consecutive no-run, no-hit games.
"The first no-hitter I had pretty good control,"
said Vander Meer, "even though I was known as
a wild man. I had a fair curve and a good sinking
ball and was always ahead of the hitters." The
second game was more of a struggle. "I threw
two or three balls to each hitter. That game I
threw only three curve balls," he said. "Until the
last inning, I wasn't going for the no-hitter—just
the shutout. I remember," said Vander Meer, "I
didn't shake off catcher Lombardi in either game
—why should I—he was calling the right
pitches."

June 15, 1949—Eddie Watikus of the Philadelphia Phillies was shot and seriously injured by a
female fan who entered his hotel room.

June 15, 1977—The New York Mets traded Tom
Seaver to the Cincinnati Reds.

June 16, 1883—The first Ladies Day in baseball
history was staged. The New York Giants granted
free admission to all women who attended on this
day.

June 16, 1916—Basketball Hall of Famer Hank Lusetti was born. He would add a new dimension to the cage sport with his one-hand shot.

June 16, 1949—Jake LaMotta defeated Marcel Cerdan in their bout in Detroit to win the middleweight boxing championship.

June 16, 1970—Chicago Bear football player Brian Piccolo died. His life story inspired the TV film "Brian's Song."

June 17, 1954—Rocky Marciano retained his heavyweight boxing crown by defeating Ezzard Charles.

June 18, 1924—George Mikan was born. He was the first of the outstanding big men in professional basketball. In 1950, he would be voted the best basketball player of the first half of the century in an AP poll.

June 18, 1939—Lou Brock was born in El Dorado, Arkansas. He would play for nineteen seasons in the major leagues, set records for the most stolen bases in a season and career and stroke 3,000 hits.

June 19, 1903—Lou Gehrig was born in New York City. Twenty years later he would play in the major leagues with the New York Yankees.

June 19, 1936—In one of the biggest upsets in boxing history, Max Schmelling of Germany recorded a twelfth round knockout of Joe Louis.

June 19, 1946—Joe Louis fought Billy Conn in a heavyweight match at Yankee Stadium. It was the first fight where tickets were sold for a hundred dollars each; it was also the first boxing match to be televised.

June 19, 1973—Hockey legend Gordie Howe signed a one-million dollar, four-year contract with the Houston Aeros of the World Hockey Association. The signing teamed Howe up with his sons, Marty and Mark.

June 20, 1960—Floyd Patterson knocked out Ingemar Johansson to become the first heavyweight boxer to regain his crown.

June 20, 1980—Roberto Duran scored a unanimous fifteen-round decision over Sugar Ray Leonard to win the World Boxing Council welterweight championship. It was the first defeat in twenty-eight professional bouts for Leonard. Duran was in control of Leonard throughout the match. "Leonard tried to pressure me," said Duran. "It didn't work. I knew I was going to win."

June 21, 1963—Bob Hayes, who would star for the Dallas Cowboys in football, ran the 100-yard dash in 9.1 to set a world record.

June 21, 1964—Jim Bunning pitched the first perfect game in the National League in eighty-four years. The Philly right-hander hurled his historic game against the New York Mets at Shea Stadium.

June 21, 1970—In soccer, Brazil won its third straight World Cup and gained permanent possession of the Jules Rimet Trophy.

June 21, 1970—Cesar Gutierrez of the Detroit Tigers became the first modern day major leaguer to notch seven hits in one game. "Sometimes you have to be lucky," said Gutierrez of the six singles and one double he recorded in his seven plate appearances against the Cleveland Indians.

June 21, 1973—Frank Leahy died. The former Notre Dame football coach from 1940 to 1954, his teams won four national championships while posting 87 wins, 11 losses and nine ties.

June 22, 1903—Carl Hubbell was born in Carthage, Missouri. He would pitch for the New York Giants for sixteen years, win 253 games, earn the nickname "the Meal Ticket" because of his dependability and be admitted to the Hall of Fame in 1947.

June 22, 1937—Joe Louis kayoed Jimmy Braddock to become heavyweight champion of the world.

June 22, 1938—Joe Louis scored a first round knockout over Max Schmelling to avenge a previous loss and retain his heavyweight title.

June 22, 1979—Troy Archer, a defensive tackle on the New York Giants, died in a traffic accident. The Giant's number one draft choice in

1976, Archer was recognized throughout the National Football League as a potential All-Pro player.

June 23, 1940—Wilma Rudolph was born. Twenty years later she would win three gold medals in Olympic track competition.

June 23, 1973—Ken Brett of the Philadelphia Phillies set a record for pitchers by recording a home run in his fourth consecutive game.

June 24, 1895—Jack Dempsey was born in Manassa, Colorado. He would be dubbed "the Manassa Mauler" because of his birthplace and his no holds barred fighting style that enabled him to become one of the great heavyweight boxing champions.

June 24, 1931—Golfing standout Billy Casper was born.

June 24, 1952—Eddie Arcaro won his 3,000th race to become the first jockey born in the United States to accomplish that feat.

June 25, 1942—Willis Reed, who would star in the NBA for the New York Knickerbockers, was born.

June 25, 1948—Joe Louis kayoed Jersey Joe Walcott in a successful defense of his heavyweight title.

June 25, 1968—Playing in his first major league game, Bobby Bonds of the San Francisco Giants whacked a grand slam home run. Bonds became the first player in history to ever accomplish this feat.

June 26, 1819—Abner Doubleday, allegedly the creator of the game of baseball, was born.

June 26, 1914—"Babe" Zaharias was born. She would be voted the top woman athlete of the first half of the 20th century.

June 26, 1959—Floyd Patterson was knocked out by Ingemar Johansson and lost his heavyweight boxing title.

June 26, 1977—Walter Kennedy died. He was National Basketball Association commissioner from 1963 to 1975.

June 27, 1913—Willie Mosconi, one of the greatest billiard players in history, was born.

June 27, 1930—The largest crowd in Wrigley Field history came out to see the Cubs play the Brooklyn Dodgers. It was Ladies Day and of the 51,556 in attendance, 30,476 were Ladies Day guests and 1,332 passholders. The official paid crowd that day was only 19,748.

June 27, 1950—Playing on a rutted field in Belo Horizonte, Brazil, the United States World Cup soccer team squeaked past a specially trained, hand-picked British team that was reportedly insured by Lloyd's of London for $3 million. The 1–0 United States victory was perhaps the greatest upset win in soccer America has ever had. The winning goal was a header in the thirty-seventh minute of the first half by Joe Gaetjens. "He was in a class by himself," Walter Bahr, now a coach at Penn State and a member of that 1950 team remembers. "He could hit awkward balls no other player could reach and still get it goalward. He was an ideal center forward."

After the goal by Gaetjens, Eddie Souza, the outside left on that 1950 World Cup team recalls, "The English bombed us. They were hitting posts and crossbar . . . they got mad and started to 'chop' us. That was their downfall. We held on to win." All the members of the United States World Cup soccer team of 1950 are now members of the National Soccer Hall of Fame.

June 27, 1972—Bobby Hull signed a ten-year contract as player-coach of the Winnipeg Jets of the World Hockey Association. The pact was reportedly valued at $3-million.

June 28, 1775—The first full scale yachting regatta was held on the Thames.

June 28, 1948—Dick Turpin defeated Vince Hawkins to win the British middleweight boxing championship. Turpin, a Jamaican, was the first black allowed to compete for a British boxing title.

June 29, 1941—Joe DiMaggio shattered George Sisler's major league record by hitting safely in his 42nd straight game. Sisler's record of 41 was set in 1922.

June 29, 1967—Primo Carnera died. On this date in 1933, Carnera defeated Jack Sharkey to win the heavyweight championship of the world.

June 30, 1970—Riverfront Stadium, a $45-million complex became the new home of the Cincinnati Reds. The new park replaced Crosley Field which the Reds had used for fifty-eight years.

June 30, 1973—Elmer Layden died. He was the 160-pound fullback in the famed "Four Horseman" backfield of Notre Dame in 1924. He went on to coach at his alma mater from 1934 to 1940.

JULY

July 1, 1859—Amherst defeated Williams College, 66–32, in what is acknowledged to be the first college baseball game.

July 1, 1951—Bob Feller of the Cleveland Indians pitched his third career no-hit game.

July 2, 1905—Jean-Rene LaCoste was born. He would become a French tennis champion and also gain fame and fortune through manufacturing tennis shirts adorned with a crocodile emblem.

July 2, 1921—More than 80,000 people paid $1,789,238 to see a heavyweight boxing match. A rough and crude Jack Dempsey was pitted against a suave and sophisticated French military hero, Georges Carpentier. The fans at Jersey City, New Jersey, who made up the "first million dollar gate" in history, were for the underdog, Carpentier. Dempsey had been advised to take it easy and give the fans a show, but in the fourth round he grew impatient and knocked out Carpentier.

July 2, 1937—Richard Perry was born. He would gain fame as an auto racer.

July 2, 1941—Joe DiMaggio batted safely in his 45th consecutive game to shatter the all-time mark of 44 straight games set by Wee Willie Keeler in 1897.

July 2, 1973—A three minute, 52 second mile— the third fastest of all time—was recorded in Stockholm, Sweden by Kenya's Ben Jipcho.

July 3, 1912—New York Giant pitcher Rube Marquard set a major league record by winning his nineteenth game in a row. In 1908, Marquard was purchased by John McGraw, of the New York Giants from the minor league Indianapolis team. The $11,000 paid for Marquard was a record sum paid for a minor leaguer at that time. Since Marquard's record with the Giants during his first three years was nine wins and eighteen losses, McGraw's judgment was criticized. Marquard was called the "$11,000 lemon." He sweetened things up for McGraw and the Giants with his nineteen consecutive victories.

July 4, 1886—Prescott, Arizona was the site of the first rodeo competition ever held.

July 4, 1914—America's first motorcycle race took place. It was a 300-mile competition staged in Dodge City, Kansas.

July 4, 1919—Jess Willard, who had defeated Jack Johnson to win the heavyweight championship of the world, met Jack Dempsey in a title match in Toledo, Ohio. Willard's championship reign was four bouts—a "no decision" and three exhibition matches. In the first round, Dempsey broke Willard's jaw; he knocked the champion down four times. At the end of round three, the 36-year-old champion's handlers threw in the towel. Dempsey became the new heavyweight champion. Willard's purse for the bout was $100,000—triple that of what Dempsey earned.

July 4, 1939—Lou Gehrig's Yankee uniform was the first to be retired. The ceremony took place before a capacity crowd at Yankee Stadium on Lou Gehrig Day.

July 5, 1947—Larry Doby became the first black to play American League baseball. Doby was inserted into the Cleveland Indians lineup in a game against the Chicago White Sox.

July 5, 1949—Monte Irvin and Hank Thompson became the first black players on the New York Giants. Their major league status made a grand total of seven black players in the big leagues. Irvin remembers the way it was: "You'd walk into a room and some people would walk out. You'd sit down on a train and one person, maybe two, would get up and walk away. This was 1949 in the United States of America. . . There was no sense of fair play. . . I do believe, however, that many of them who were prejudiced were sorry afterward that they behaved that way."

July 6, 1912—Stockholm, Sweden was the site of the Olympic Games in which Jim Thorpe proved to all that he was the world's greatest athlete.

July 6, 1933—The first home run ever hit in an All-Star game was appropriately enough recorded by Babe Ruth.

July 6, 1935—Helen Wills Moody notched her seventh women's singles title in the Wimbledon tennis tournament.

July 6, 1938—Johnny Vander Meer pleased the hometown crowd in Cincinnati by hurling three fine innings to help pace his National League team to a 4–1 win over the American League in the All-Star game.

July 6, 1941—More than 60,000 spectators watched as the New York Yankees dedicated a monument to Lou Gehrig at the Stadium.

July 6, 1942—The American League nipped the National League, 3–1, in the annual All-Star game. Lou Boudreau and Rudy York hit home runs for the victors that accounted for all the American League scoring; Mickey Owen hit a pinch-hit, eighth inning home run for the National League.

July 6, 1957—Althea Gibson became the first black to record a victory in the Wimbledon singles competition.

July 6, 1975—A $350,000 match race between Foolish Pleasure and Ruffian ended in tragedy. Ruffian broke her right front leg while in the lead just before the half-mile marker in the mile-and-a-quarter race. Ruffian was later destroyed.

July 7, 1902—John J. McGraw left the Baltimore Orioles and joined the New York Giants as manager. He remained for thirty years and led the Giants to ten pennants.

July 7, 1948—Leroy Robert Paige, better known as Satchel Paige, arrived on the major league baseball scene as a rookie pitcher for the Cleveland Indians. He gave his official age as 42; Satchel won six games that year, lost but one and compiled a fine 2.48 earned-run-average. A longtime star in the Negro Leagues, there are estimates that he pitched thirty-three and won more than 2,000 games. He claimed that the secret of his success was that "Even though I got old, my arm stayed young."

July 7, 1936—The National League won an All-Star game, for the first time defeating the American League, 4–3. Joe Medwick's single in the fifth inning proved the NL margin of victory. Carl Hubbell and Dizzy Dean pitched three shutout innings each.

July 7, 1937—Paced by four RBI's by Lou Gehrig and his third inning home run, the American League rolled to an 8–3 victory over the National League in the fifth All-Star game. A line drive hit by Earl Averill broke Dizzy Dean's toe. The injury proved to be a turning point in the Cardinal right-hander's career. He attempted to return to pitching too soon and, favoring the injured foot, developed a sore arm and lost his fluid pitching motion.

July 7, 1959—The National League defeated the American League, 5–4, in the All-Star game played at Pittsburgh. Hank Aaron batted in the tying run and scored the winning run. Al Kaline and Eddie Mathews hit home runs.

July 7, 1964—Johnny Callison's three-run homer in the bottom of the ninth inning gave the National League a 7–4 win over the American League in the All-Star game. Cepeda's bloop single had set the stage for the Callison home run and had scored Willie Mays with the game tying run.

July 8, 1889—The last bare-knuckle title fight in American history took place. John L. Sullivan outlasted Jake Kilrain in a bout that lasted seventy-five rounds.

July 8, 1924—The Phillies set a major league baseball record by playing in a doubleheader that involved 25 innings of errorless baseball on their part.

July 8, 1935—The American League defeated the National League, 4–1, in the third All-Star game. Three RBI's by Jimmy Foxx and the three-hit, six inning pitching of Lefty Gomez aided the victors.

July 8, 1941—In the first All-Star game played at Detroit, a three-run homer by Ted Williams in the bottom of the ninth inning gave the American League a 7–5 victory. Arky Vaughan set an All-Star game record by hitting two home runs.

July 8, 1942—World War II demands affected the sports of automobile and motorcycle racing. The Office of Defense Transportation banned all racing after July 31, 1941 until the war's end as a means of conserving rubber.

July 8, 1947—In the All-Star game played in Chicago, the American League eked out a 2–1 win over the National League. A Johnny Mize home run was the only scoring until the sixth inning when the American League scored on a double play ball by Joe DiMaggio. A throwing error by Johnny Sain in the seventh inning set up the scoring of the American League's go ahead run.

July 8, 1952—At Palmerston, New Zealand, the shortest fight on record took place. Ross Cleverly knocked down D. Emerson with his first punch. The referee stopped the fight at seven seconds of that first round.

July 8, 1952—Rain ended the All-Star game after five innings in Philadelphia. A Hank Sauer two-run homer in the fourth inning was the margin in the 3–2 National League victory.

July 8, 1958—A pinch-hit single by Gil McDougald in the sixth inning scored Frank Malzone and gave the American League a 4–3 win over the National League in the All-Star game played at Baltimore. It was the first All-Star game in which an extra base hit was not made.

July 9, 1946—In five trips to the plate, Ted Williams of the Boston Red Sox had one of the most productive days ever experienced by a batter in an All-Star Game. Williams recorded two home runs, two singles, drove in five runs and scored four more. He also walked.

July 9, 1947—Orenthal James Simpson, better known as O.J. Simpson, was born. A great collegiate star at USC, Simpson went pro with Buffalo in 1972 and became the first player in history to rush for more than 2,000 yards in a season.

July 9, 1957—At St. Louis, the American League defeated the National League, 6–5, in the All-Star game. Both teams scored three times in the ninth inning. A running catch by Minnie Minoso of a shot hit by Gil Hodges closed out the National League rally.

July 9, 1963—The National League won the All-Star game played at Cleveland, 5–3. It was a nostalgic event. Stan Musial appeared in his 24th All-Star game to set a record. And Mickey Mantle—though unable to participate because of a broken foot—was complimented by the players who named him the starting centerfielder. Willie Mays proved to be the all-star of All Stars. He stole two bases, scored two runs, batted in two runs and made a sensational catch up against the centerfield fence stopping a Joe Pepitone bid for an extra base hit.

July 9, 1967—Dick Allen homered over the centerfield fence between the flagpole and the stands at Connie Mack Stadium. He became the

first player in history to accomplish that feat
since the fence was raised to thirty-two feet in
1934.

July 9, 1968—The National League won the first
1–0 game in All-Star competition. The senior
circuit run was scored by Willie Mays who came
across the plate in the first inning on a double
play ball. A five strikeout performance by Tom
Seaver highlighted the National League's three-
hit pitching performance by Drysdale, Marichal,
Carlton, Reed and Koosman. It was the first indoor All-Star game ever played—the site, the
Astrodome in Houston, Texas.

July 9, 1973—Tel Aviv, Israel was the site of the
ninth Maccabiah Games. The competition
named for Judas Maccabeus, a Jewish guerilla
leader, originated in 1929 in Czechoslavakia. The
1973 games were dedicated to the eleven Israeli
athletes murdered at the Munich Olympics in
1972.

July 9, 1980—The National League defeated the
American League, 4–2, to win its ninth straight
All-Star Game. The contest was played at Los
Angeles before 56,088, a Dodger Stadium record
crowd. "If we played more than once," said Red
Sox catcher Carlton Fisk, "it would be more of a
contest." Fisk struck out twice in the game—the
American League's seventeenth loss in the last
eighteen All Star contests.

July 10, 1934—Carl Hubbell thrilled Giant fans
and National League rooters at the All-Star game

held at the Polo Grounds. The Hall of Fame pitcher struck out Babe Ruth, Lou Gehrig and Jimmy Foxx of the American League in the first inning of the game.

July 10, 1940—The first shutout in All-Star game competition was recorded. The National League defeated the American League, 4-0, at St. Louis. Derringer, Walters, Wyatt, French and Hubbell combined their pitching talents for the shutout. National League manager Bill McKechnie went on to lead the Reds to the World Series championship.

July 10, 1943—Arthur Ashe was born. He would become the first black to gain fame and fortune in men's tennis.

July 10, 1951—Sugar Ray Robinson was defeated by Randy Turpin and lost his world middleweight title. It was only the second loss for Robinson in 133 bouts.

July 10, 1951—Six home runs were hit to set a new record as the National League defeated the American League, 8-3, and won back-to-back All Star games for the first time. Musial, Elliot, Kiner and Hodges homered for the winners; Wertz and Kell hit home runs for the American League.

July 10, 1956—Back-to-back homers in the sixth inning by Ted Williams and Mickey Mantle were not enough as the National League defeated the American League, 7-3, in the annual All-Star game. Ken Boyer's three hits and three excellent plays in the field were key factors in the NL win.

July 10, 1962—Roberto Clemente's three hits sparked the National League to a 3–1 victory over the American League in the All-Star game played at Washington. Maury Wills scored two of the three NL runs.

July 11, 1914—Babe Ruth made his major league debut as a pitcher with the Boston Red Sox. Cleveland first baseman Jack Graney, the first major leaguer to wear a number on his uniform and the first to broadcast games, was the first batter Ruth faced.

July 11, 1916—The legendary horse Dan Patch died. The only world-champion harness-racing horse never to have lost a race, Dan Patch set a record in 1905 for pacing the mile that stood until 1938. During his career, the name Dan Patch became synonymous with "racehorse." People flocked to see him just to catch a glimpse of him *en route* to and from the track. He earned more than $3 million dollars for his owners which was a great deal of money for that time. There was Dan Patch chewing-tobacco; there were Dan Patch cigars, pillows, and washing machines. People even danced the Dan Patch two-step. At the time of his retirement in 1909, Dan Patch held nine world records. The day after his death, Dan Patch's owner died, too. Heart ailments were the cause of death for both horse and owner.

July 11, 1939—The American League defeated the National League, 3–1, in the second All-Star game played in New York City. Bob Feller saved the game for the American League. He came in with the bases loaded in the sixth inning and one out and forced Arky Vaughan to hit into a rally-killing double play. Joe DiMaggio recorded his only All-Star game home run.

July 11, 1944—Phil Cavaretta put on a show in the All-Star game that earned him a place in the record books. The Chicago Cub reached base five times via three walks, a triple and a single. The National League defeated the American League, 7–1. A four-run fifth inning locked up the game for the victors.

July 11, 1950—A 14th inning home run by Red Schoendienst gave the National League a 4–3 win over the American League in the All-Star game played in Chicago. Ted Williams was a casualty of the game. He broke his elbow in the first inning while catching the ball against the left field wall. He was unable to play for the Red Sox until the end of the season. Eleven pitchers appeared in the game.

July 11, 1960—Willie Mays slammed a single, double and triple to key a twelve-hit National League 5–3 All-Star game victory over the American League at Kansas City. Banks, Crandall, Musial, Ken Boyer and Al Kaline hit home runs.

July 11, 1961—The National League scored a 5–4 victory over the American League in the All-

Star game played at San Francisco. Roberto Clemente, Willie Mays and Hank Aaron all figured prominently in the win. Mays had tied the game by driving in Aaron with a double, and Clemente won the game with a tenth inning single. A total of seven errors was committed to set an All-Star game record.

July 11, 1967—The longest All-Star game in history finally ended in the 15th inning. Tony Perez homered to give the National League a 2–1 victory. The only other scoring in the game came on Richie Allen's second inning home run and a homer by Brooks Robinson in the sixth. Thirty batters struck out—six of them victims of Ferguson Jenkins who tied the record set by Carl Hubbell and Johnny Vander Meer. The five American League pitchers did not allow a walk.

July 11, 1978—The National League won its seventh consecutive All-Star game defeating the American League, 7–3, at San Diego. A tie-breaking triple by Steve Garvey keyed the NL win.

July 12, 1947—Soviet Olympic eligibility was established as the Russians substituted medals for cash for its nationals competitors, thus making them able to participate.

July 12, 1949—The American League defeated the National League, 11–7, in the first All-Star game ever played in Brooklyn. A total of twenty-five hits were recorded at the Ebbets Field ball park. Musial homered in an All-Star game for the second year in a row. It was the first All-Star game that blacks appeared in. Jackie Robinson, Roy Campanella and Don Newcombe were on the National League roster; Larry Doby played for the American League.

July 12, 1949—The groundwork was laid by major league club owners to increase safety on the baseball field. An agreement stated that, beginning with the 1950 season, all parks would establish paths made of cinder in front of all outfield walls to warn an outfielder of danger and cut down on injuries.

July 12, 1955—Stan Musial and Gene Conley starred in the National League's twelve inning come-from-behind All-Star game victory over the American League in Milwaukee. Musial's homer was the margin in the 6–5 NL win; Conley pitched the bottom of the twelfth inning and struck out the side.

July 12, 1966—The All-Star game was played in 105° heat in St. Louis. The National League won, 2–1, in ten innings. The hometown fans were made happy when Cardinal catcher Tim McCarver scored the winning run coming home on a single by Maury Wills. Denny McLain's three perfect innings and Brooks Robinson's three hits were American League bright spots.

July 13, 1896—Big Ed Delahanty of the Philadelphia Phillies pounded four home runs in one game to become only the second major leaguer to accomplish that feat. One of four baseball playing brothers, Ed had a lifetime batting average of .346 and won a batting title in both the National and American League.

July 13, 1908—Great Britain's King Edward VII presided over the opening of the Olympics in London.

July 13, 1943—The first night All-Star game was played. Bobby Doerr's three-run homer paced the 5–3 American League victory. Vince DiMaggio collected a home run, a triple and a single. The game was played amidst the backdrop of World War II combat; United States servicemen heard the game over shortwave radio all over the world.

July 13, 1948—Although top American League stars DiMaggio, Williams, Newhouser and Kell were not in action, the junior loop managed to defeat the National League, 5–2. Musial homered for the losers; Hoot Evers homered for the victors.

July 13, 1954—The American League broke a five-year All-Star game losing streak. It defeated the National League, 11–9, in the game played at Cleveland that was the highest scoring All-Star contest in history. A two-run, eighth inning single by Nellie Fox won the game for the American League. Quite a few records were set: most hits by one team (17) for the American League; most hits by two teams (31); five RBI's and two home runs recorded by Al Rosen tied an All-Star game record.

July 13, 1960—Six National League pitchers scattered eight hits as the senior circuit scored a 6–0 victory over the American League in the All-Star game played at Yankee Stadium. Willie Mays rapped out three hits, including a home run.

July 13, 1965—Five home runs were hit in the All-Star game as the National League hung on to win, 6–5, in the game played at Minnesota. The crucial play in the contest came in the eighth inning. Willie Mays made a leaping, backhanded stab and catch of a fly ball hit by Jimmy Hall to end an American League rally. Mays had misplayed the ball but recovered.

July 13, 1971—Frank Robinson became the first player in All-Star game history to hit a home run for each league. The American League won an All-Star game for the first time since 1962. In addition to Robinson, there were five other players in the 6–4 AL victory who hit home runs. One of them was Hank Aaron who recorded his first All-Star game homer.

July 13, 1972—Two National Football League franchises were traded: Carroll Rosenbloom swapped his entire Baltimore Colts team to Los Angeles owner Robert Irsay for the L.A. Rams club.

July 13, 1976—The National League's 100th anniversary was celebrated with the All-Star game played at Philadelphia. The senior circuit won, 7–1. It was the fifth straight National League All-

Star triumph and thirteenth win in the last fourteen games. Five NL pitchers held the American
League to five hits.

July 14, 1946—Behind three home runs and
eight runs batted in by Ted Williams, the Boston
Red Sox outlasted the Cleveland Indians, 11–10,
in the first game of a doubleheader. The
"Boudreau Shift" was devised by Cleveland
manager Lou Boudreau for the second game of
the doubleheader. He positioned all hit fielders
but his left fielder on the right side of the
diamond. The left fielder took up a position in
left centerfield. The maneuver was aimed at cut-
ting down the pull hitting power of Williams.

July 14, 1951—The Molly Pitcher Handicap at
Monmouth Park in New Jersey was televised in
color by CBS. It was the first sports event to get
the color TV treatment.

July 14, 1953—The National League defeated
the American League, 5–3, in the All-Star game
at Cincinnati. Enos Slaughter of the St. Louis
Cardinals was the star of the game. He scored
two runs, drove in another and had two hits; his
diving grab of a line drive by Harvey Kuenn was
the fielding play of the game.

July 14, 1968—Hank Aaron whacked the 500th
home run of his career. He became the eighth
player in history to record this milestone.

July 14, 1970—It was the first time since 1957
that fans voted for the players in the All-Star

game. It did not make too much difference to the National League as they won for the eighth straight time. It took the NL twelve innings to do it but, after trailing 4-1 going into the ninth inning and tying the game, a Pete Rose single won it for the senior circuit in the twelfth.

July 15, 1912—The Olympic Games in Stockholm, Sweden concluded. Jim Thorpe won the decathlon. In the closing ceremonies, Sweden's King Gustav proclaimed Thorpe the world's greatest athlete.

July 15, 1973—Nolan Ryan of the California Angels pitched his second no-hitter of the season —a 2-0 win over the Detroit Tigers. Ryan became one of the few pitchers in history to hurl two no-hitters in one season.

July 15, 1975—For the twelfth time in the last thirteen games played, the National League defeated the American League in the All-Star competition. Top AL pitchers Catfish Hunter and Rich Gossage were shelled for three runs in the ninth inning to break a 3-3 tie and give the National League their 6-3 victory. All the American League runs came in on a Carl Yastremski three-run home run. Jon Matlack of the New York Mets was the winning pitcher.

July 15, 1976—Jimmy Dykes died. He gave to baseball a half century of playing and managing skill.

July 16, 1947—Rocky Graziano defeated Tony Zale for the middleweight boxing title. The bout, held in Chicago, grossed close to half a million dollars—a record to that point in time for an indoor boxing match.

July 16, 1950—The largest crowd to ever witness a sporting event in person came out to see Brazil play soccer against Uruguay. The site of the game was Maracana Municipal Stadium, Rio de Janeiro, Brazil.

July 16, 1956—The Detroit Tigers were sold to an eleven-member syndicate for $5,500,000—a record sum to that point in time for a baseball franchise.

July 16, 1970—Three Rivers Stadium, the new home of the Pittsburgh Pirates, was officially opened. Cincinnati defeated Pittsburgh, 3–2.

July 17, 1917—Lou Boudreau was born in Harvey, Illinois. Twenty-five years later he would become the player-manager of the Cleveland Indians, the youngest pilot in baseball. Fifty-three years later he would be admitted to the Hall of Fame.

July 17, 1941—Joe DiMaggio's consecutive game-hitting streak was stopped at 56.

July 17, 1954—The Brooklyn Dodgers fielded a team that had more black players on it than whites. It was the first time in baseball history that such an event took place.

July 17, 1961—Ty Cobb died in Atlanta, Georgia. A baseball immortal, Cobb played twenty-two seasons for the Detroit Tigers and two more for the Philadelphia Athletics. He also managed Detroit in the years 1921–1926. Cobb compiled a lifetime batting average of .367, stole 892 bases, and won twelve batting titles in a span of thirteen years. By the time he retired, he had set ninety individual records. Cobb was born in Narrows, Georgia and called "The Georgia Peach."

July 17, 1974—Dizzy Dean died. One of baseball's most colorful characters, Dean won 150 games against 83 losses in a too short Hall of Fame pitching career.

July 17, 1979—The National League defeated the American League, 7–6, to win its eighth straight All-Star game. Dave Parker, who made two game-saving throws in the contest played at Seattle, was selected for the Most Valuable Player award.

July 18, 1927—Ty Cobb recorded his 4,000th hit, thus becoming the first and only player ever to accomplish that historic feat.

July 18, 1929—Dick Button, who would become a fabled name in world figure skating, was born.

July 18, 1940—Joe Torre was born in Brooklyn, New York. He would star with several National League teams and become the manager of the New York Mets.

July 18, 1951—Jersey Joe Walcott kayoed Ezzard Charles to win the heavyweight championship of the world. It was Walcott's fifth attempt at the title.

July 18, 1970—Willie Mays became the tenth player in major league history to record his 3,000th hit.

July 19, 1909—The first unassisted triple play in baseball history was executed by Neal Ball, Cleveland Indian shortstop.

July 19, 1914—The Boston Braves began their march from last place in the National League to first by winning 61 of their last 77 games. This accomplishment was only part of what earned the Braves their reputation as a "miracle team." In the World Series, the Braves were given no chance to defeat a powerful Philadelphia Athletics team. However, the Braves won the series and became the first team to ever sweep four straight games.

July 19, 1965—The San Francisco Giants signed pitcher Warren Spahn as a free agent.

July 19, 1977—Jim Palmer—one of the best pitchers in the American League—was shelled for four runs in the first inning as the National League went on to a 7–5 All-Star game victory. Joe Morgan and Greg Luzinski homered in the first to spearhead the NL attack. It was the sixth straight win for the National League in All-Star game competition.

July 20, 1859—Fans paid fifty cents each to see a game between Brooklyn and New York at the

Fashion Race Course in Long Island. It was the first admission charge ever for a baseball game.

July 20, 1954—Tennis champion Mo Connoly had her right leg crushed in a horseback riding accident.

July 21, 1957—Althea Gibson became the first black to win a major United States tennis championship. Ms. Gibson won the women's national clay court title.

July 21, 1967—Hall of Famer Jimmy Foxx died in Miami, Florida, at the age of 59. During his baseball days he had two nicknames. His main one, "Double X," was derived from the last two letters of his last name. He was also known as "the Beast," which indicated the way his rivals viewed his playing ability. Foxx averaged better than a hit a game in a twenty-year career, compiling a .325 batting average and a .609 slugging percentage. He hit 534 homers, scored over 1,700 runs and drove in almost 2,000 runs.

July 21, 1973—Hank Aaron of the Atlanta Braves recorded his 700th career home run in a game against Philadelphia.

July 21, 1976—Earle Combs died. He played a dozen seasons for the New York Yankees and recorded a lifetime batting average of .350. He was known as the man who batted ahead of Babe Ruth and Lou Gehrig in the "Murderers' Row" batting order.

July 22, 1963—Sonny Liston knocked out Floyd Patterson in the first round of their bout at Las Vegas in a successful defense of his heavyweight crown.

July 23, 1919—Harold Henry Reese was born. He would be known as "Pee Wee" because of his small size and childhood skill with marbles. Fifteen years a Dodger, Reese wore #1 on his uniform and was number one for millions of baseball fans.

July 23, 1936—Don Drysdale was born in Van Nuys, California. A fire-balling, right-handed pitcher, he starred for fourteen seasons for the Dodgers of Brooklyn and then the Dodgers of Los Angeles.

July 23, 1969—Baseball's hundredth anniversary was celebrated with the All-Star game played in Washington. Willie McCovey of the San Francisco Giants slammed two home runs and drove in four runs to torque the NL 9–3 win —its seventh in a row over the American League. A homer and a couple of RBI's by Johnny Bench helped supplement the eleven-hit National League attack off seven American League pitchers.

July 23, 1974—Los Angeles Dodger first baseman Steve Garvey was the standout player in the All-Star game played at Pittsburgh. Garvey, whose name was not even listed on the All-Star ballot, doubled, singled, scored a run and drove in another and also made some excellent fielding plays to pace the 7–2 National League victory.

July 24, 1966—Golfer Tony Lema was killed in a plane crash near Lansing, Michigan.

July 24, 1969—Hoyt Wilhelm, who began his major league pitching career in 1952, made his 907th appearance and set an all-time record. Wilhelm closed out his twenty-one-year career in 1972 with his 1,070th pitching appearance, a record that probably will never be broken.

July 24, 1973—National League power crushed the American League in the All-Star game played at Kansas City. Bench, Bonds and Davis pounded homers for the National League in its 7–1 win. A record 54 players were used, 28 of them by the National League.

July 25, 1940—Track and field star John Pennel was born. He would become the first person to pole vault above seventeen feet.

July 25, 1972—Hank Aaron thrilled the home town Atlanta fans by hitting a two-run home run in the All-Star game. The National League edged the American League, 4–3, in ten innings. It was the seventh extra inning All-Star game and the seventh extra inning All-Star game victory for the National League.

July 26, 1923—Hoyt Wilhem was born. Fifty years later he would still be pitching in the major leagues.

July 26, 1948—Babe Ruth made his last public appearance. He attended a New York City premiere of the "Babe Ruth Story."

July 27, 1905—Leo Durocher was born in Springfield, Massachusetts. He would play in the major leagues for seventeen years and spend twenty-four more years as a controversial manager for the New York Giants, the Brooklyn Dodgers, Chicago Cubs and Houston Astros.

July 27, 1965—Robin Lee Graham, age 16, became the youngest person ever to make a voyage alone by sloop around the world. She sailed with her two kittens from San Pedro, California on the 24-foot-sloop, Dove. On April 30, 1970, she completed her 33,000 mile trip in Los Angeles.

July 28, 1943—Bill Bradley was born. He would become a star forward for the New York Knickerbockers of the National Basketball Association and be elected United States Senator from New Jersey.

July 29, 1870—George Dixon was born. Dubbed "Little Chocolate," he was the first black bantamweight and featherweight boxer.

July 29, 1936—The Boston Red Sox became the first baseball team to use an airplane to fly from one major league city to another. The Red Sox flew from St. Louis to Chicago. Five players refused to participate.

July 30, 1928—Joe Nuxhall was born in Hamilton, Ohio. In June of 1944, at the age of fifteen years, ten months and eleven days, he became a member of the Cincinnati Reds and the youngest major league player of all time.

July 30, 1959—Willie McCovey of the San Francisco Giants rapped four hits in four at bats in his major league debut.

July 30, 1962—The American League defeated the National League, 9–4, in the annual All-Star game. A couple of double plays executed by the American League and four National League errors helped the junior circuit to its win.

July 30, 1966—The largest gate receipts for one soccer game—$573,454—were collected for a World Cup Final at Empire Stadium, Wembley, Greater London; England played against West Germany.

July 30, 1968—Shortstop Ron Hansen of the Washington Senators became the eighth player in major league history to record an unassisted triple play. Three days later he was traded to the Chicago White Sox.

July 30, 1977—Carlos Monzon outpointed Rodrigo Valdez and retired as middleweight champion of the world. He was thirty-four years old and had defended his title fourteen times. "I think I showed everyone I am one of the great ones," Monzon said. "But it's over now. I'm going to start living like a human being." He was one of the great ones. Monzon won his last thirty-two fights; during his career he was unbeaten in seventy-three straight fights while drawing nine others.

July 31, 1954—Joe Adcock of the Milwaukee Braves pounded four home runs and a double against the Dodgers. His eighteen total bases in that one game set a major league record.

July 31, 1961—Rain wiped out the All-Star game played at Boston. It was the first time in the history of the event that this had happened. Both teams were tied, 1–1, after nine innings when the rains came.

AUGUST

August 1, 1936—Berlin, Germany was the site for the opening of the Olympic Games. Adolph Hitler presided over the festivities.

August 1, 1950—Curt Simmons of the Philadelphia Phillies was called to active military duty. The star southpaw became the first major leaguer to become a participant in the Korean War.

August 1, 1959—French racing car driving champion Jean Behra died in an accident in Berlin.

August 2, 1935—By committing three errors in the first inning, Dolf Camilli of the Phillies set a record for first baseman. The Phillies lost the game to the Dodgers, 8–3.

August 2, 1937—Billy Cannon was born; twenty-two years later he would win the Heisman Trophy as the outstanding collegiate football player of 1959.

August 2, 1978—Pete Rose, bidding to break Joe DiMaggio's consecutive game hitting streak of 56, had his streak stopped at 44. "The pitcher tried too hard," said Rose.

August 3, 1921—Baseball Commissioner Landis mandated that even though acquitted, the players on the Chicago White Sox charged with fixing the 1919 World Series be barred from organized baseball for life.

August 3, 1949—The National Basketball Association (NBA) came into existence as a result of the merger of the Basketball Association of America and the National Basketball League.

August 3, 1959—A second 1959 All-Star game was played. The site was Los Angeles. The American League won, 5–3, on a fourth inning single by Nellie Fox of the Chicago White Sox. Frank Malzone, Yogi Berra, Rocky Colavito, Frank Robinson and Junior Gilliam all hit home runs.

August 4, 1921—Maurice "the Rocket" Richard was born. He would become one of the legendary players in the National Hockey League. Scorer of 544 lifetime goals, the first to notch fifty goals in one season, a talented, brawling player, he is especially well remembered by former star goalkeeper Glenn Hall. "What I remember most of all about the Rocket was his eyes. When he came flying toward you with the puck on his stick, his eyes were all lit up, flashing and gleaming like a pinball machine. It was terrifying."

August 4, 1957—Florence Chadwick swam the English Channel in six hours and seven minutes —a record time.

August 5, 1921—Baseball's first radio broadcast took place over KDKA. Pittsburgh defeated the Phillies, 8–5. Harold Arlin was the announcer.

August 5, 1955—It was announced that the Brooklyn Dodgers would play eight games in 1956 in Jersey City, New Jersey.

August 5, 1960—The first reported trade of major league managers took place. Detroit manager Jimmy Dykes was traded for Cleveland manager Joe Gordon.

August 6, 1890—Cy Young recorded his first major league appearance as a pitcher for Cleveland in a game against the White Sox. Young also notched the first of his record 511 wins.

August 6, 1926—Gertrude Ederle, age 19, swam the English Channel from Cape Gris-Nez, France to Kingsdown, England. She swam the Channel in fourteen hours and thirty-one minutes.

August 6, 1955—Ron Davis was born in Houston, Texas. He grew up to be a 6'4" hard-throwing right-hander. In 1979, he won his first eight decisions as a member of the New York Yankees and finished the season with a 14–2 record.

August 6, 1960—Bob Mathias won the decathlon in the Olympic Games staged in London.

August 7, 1900—Race horse trainer Sunny Jim Fitzsimmons had more than 2,000 winners in a fifty-year career. On this day at New York's Brighton Beach track, Agnes D., a horse trained by Fitzsimmons, won the race. It was the first of Fitzsimmons' more than 2,000 winners.

August 7, 1929—Don Larsen was born. He would gain a place in the record books by pitching the first perfect game in World Series history.

August 8, 1923—Esther Williams was born. She would become a championship swimmer and a movie box office draw.

August 8, 1934—Wilbert Robinson died in Atlanta, Georgia. Seventeen years a major league player, nineteen years a manager, he was elected to the Hall of Fame in 1945.

August 8, 1936—Don Bowden was born. He would become the first American to run a mile in under four minutes.

August 9, 1928—This was the birth date of Bob Cousy who would become perhaps the greatest ball handler in the history of the National Basketball Association. From 1953–1960, Cousy led the NBA in assists.

August 9, 1936—Jesse Owens became the first United States athlete to win four Olympic gold medals. Owens, a black man, recorded the feat despite the hostilities of the Nazis at the Olympics held in Berlin.

August 9, 1946—The entire major league baseball schedule was played at night. It was the first time in the history of the sport that this took place.

August 9, 1969—George Preston Marshall, President Emeritus of the Washington Redskins, died at the age of 72.

August 10, 1963—Dick Tiger retained his middleweight title by defeating Gene Fullmer. The bout was the first championship fight ever held in Nigeria.

August 11, 1951—The first color TV transmission of baseball took place. WCBS-TV broadcasted a doubleheader between the Boston Braves and the Brooklyn Dodgers.

August 12, 1964—Mickey Mantle of the New York Yankees, for the tenth time in his career, pounded home runs in one game batting left-handed and right-handed.

August 13, 1919—Legendary race horse Man o'War lost a race for the first and only time in his career. The horse that won the Sanford Memorial Stakes at Saratoga, New York and defeated Man o' War was named Upset.

August 13, 1948—The "Ageless Wonder" Satchel Paige, after a career that made him a legend in the Negro Leagues, was given his first major league start. Paige pitched the Cleveland Indians to 5–0 victory over the Chicago White Sox.

He didn't walk anyone and only gave up five singles.

August 13, 1972—George Weiss died. As Yankee general manager he presided over a dynasty that saw the Bronx Bombers win seven world series and ten American League pennants.

August 14, 1936—For the first time in Olympic history, basketball was on the program. The USA defeated Canada, 19–8, to win the gold medal.

August 14, 1971—St. Louis Cardinal righthander Bob Gibson hurled a no-hitter against the Pirates. It was the first no-hitter pitched at Forbes Field in Pittsburgh in sixty-one years.

August 15, 1954—Bob Toski won the Tam O' Shanter golf tournament. He collected a record $50,000 in prize money and another $50,000 for a golf exhibition contract.

August 16, 1930—Frank Gifford was born. He would star in football for the New York Giants and become even better known as a TV sportscaster.

August 16, 1948—Babe Ruth died in Memorial Hospital in Manhattan. He had been ailing for a while, and his death was expected. It sent the nation into mourning. Perhaps the greatest slugger of all-time and also one of baseball's most colorful characters, Ruth's accomplishments and his personality combined to help make baseball the national pastime.

August 17, 1938—Henry Armstrong defeated Lou Ambers for the lightweight championship. Armstrong became the first boxer to hold three titles at the same time.

August 18, 1934—Roberto Clemente, who would star for eighteen years for the Pittsburgh Pirates, was born in Carolina, Puerto Rico.

August 18, 1973—Hank Aaron stroked his 1,378th extra base hit—a new major league record.

August 19, 1931—Willie Shoemaker was born. He weighed just 2½ pounds. He grew up to be just a bit less than five feet tall, just a bit less than 100 pounds—and one of the most successful jockeys in history.

August 19, 1951—Baseball has had a history of many zany moments, but one of its zaniest took place when Eddie Gaedel came to bat for the St. Louis Browns against the Detroit Tigers. Gaedel wore number 1/8. He was a midget, only three feet, seven inches tall. The little man walked on four straight pitches and then was replaced by a pinch runner.

August 19, 1957—The Board of Directors of the New York Giants voted to move the team to San Francisco in 1958.

August 20, 1923—An amateur was defined by the International Amateur Federation as any person who competed solely for the love of sport.

August 20, 1936—Wilt Chamberlain was born. From his rookie year (1959–60) on in the National Basketball Association, Chamberlain was a dominant force. He had a 30.1 lifetime scoring average and once scored 100 points in a single game. Dubbed "The Stilt," he towered over his peers in size and ability and will be remembered as perhaps the greatest offensive player in the history of the league. On the negative side, he was probably one of the poorest foul shooters in NBA history: he set negative foul shooting records: most foul shots missed in a game (18); most foul shots missed in a season (528); most foul shots missed in a playoff game (17). His foul shooting was so poor that it was a strategy technique on the part of some teams to foul him and take their chances with Wilt on the foul line rather than allow him to take a shot from the field. Chamberlain was NBA Most Valuable Player four times and an all-star game without an appearance by him was an oddity.

August 20, 1948—One week after he had shut out the White Sox of Chicago, Satchel Paige took the mound for his second major league start before 78,382. It was the largest crowd to ever witness a night baseball game. Paige pitched a 1–0, three-hit shutout, relying on what he called "bat dodgers." He also threw some fast balls and hesitation pitches.

August 20, 1951—American League president Will Harridge banned the St. Louis Browns from using midget Eddie Gaedel in any more baseball games.

August 20, 1967—Detroit trimmed the Chargers, 38–17, in the first game ever played in the 50,000-seat San Diego Stadium.

August 20, 1968—Jockey immortal Earl Sande died. Among his accomplishments were three Kentucky Derby wins.

August 21, 1929—For the first time in history a professional football team trained for a new season in a site other than its home town. On this date the Chicago Cardinals began their training for the 1929 season at Coldwater, Michigan.

August 21, 1971—Laura Baugh, age 16, won the United States women's amateur golf tourney. She became the youngest golfer in history to accomplish that feat.

August 22, 1851—The first international yacht race was won by a United States schooner named "America." It defeated fourteen British yachts. The race was a part of the ceremonies of the London Exposition of that year. The Royal Yacht Club of England donated a trophy originally called the Hundred-Guinea Cup that was to go to the winner of the race around the Isle of Wight. The British were not too impressed when the "America" won the race and maintained that in "due time" they would win back the cup then valued at $500. That 1851 race has evolved into a series of international races for twelve-meter yachts. More than $75,000,000 had been spent in attempting to win the cup named for the vessel named for the nation that originally won the trophy. And the America's Cup still remains—as it always has—in the United States.

August 22, 1951—More than 75,000 fans watched the Harlem Globetrotters in action at Berlin's Olympic Stadium. It was the largest attendance at that point in time for a basketball game.

August 23, 1936—Bob Feller, in his major league pitching debut for the Cleveland Indians, struck out the first eight men to face him and then seven more for a total of fifteen—one short of the then league record.

August 23, 1942—Nancy Richey, who would star in tennis in the 1960's, was born.

August 24, 1912—Thousands cheered as Jim Thorpe and other Olympic athletes paraded through the streets of New York City.

August 24, 1963—The two-minute mark in the 200-meter freestyle was broken for the first time. Don Schollander's winning time at Osaka, Japan was 1:58.4.

August 25, 1920—Ethelda Bleibtrey became the first American woman to win a medal in Olympic competition. Ms. Bleibtrey was the victor in the 100-meter freestyle held in Antwerp, Belgium.

August 26, 1939—The doubleheader between the Dodgers and the Reds from Ebbets Field was the first baseball game ever televised. NBC transmitted the action with Red Barber as the announcer.

August 26, 1943—At the Polo Grounds in New York City, 38,000 fans came out to see a game between twenty-six players from the Brooklyn Dodgers, New York Giants and New York Yankees—billed as the War Bond All-Stars—and a team of Army baseball stars. Enos Slaughter of the Cardinals, Hank Greenberg of the Tigers and Sid Hudson of the Senators were among the players on the Army baseball team. The War Bond All-Stars won, 5–2.

August 26, 1947—Dan Bankhead of the Brooklyn Dodgers became the first black pitcher to appear in a major league game. Bankhead also stroked a home run in his first major league at bat.

August 26, 1955—The first color transmission of a tennis tournament took place; the Davis Cup from Forest Hills, New York was carried by NBC.

August 26, 1961—The National Hockey League Hall of Fame Building was officially opened by John F. Diefenbaker, Prime Minister of Canada.

August 26, 1973—St. Louis Cardinal superstar Lou Brock stole his fiftieth base of the 1973 season. The steal, Brock's ninth straight year of fifty or more, broke Ty Cobb's record of eight straight years of fifty or more stolen bases.

August 27, 1921—A professional football franchise was granted to Green Bay, Wisconsin. The sum of $500 was contributed to the new team for equipment and uniforms by the Indian Packing Company. And with the money came the team's nickname, the Packers, and permission to use the packing company field for practice.

August 27, 1951—Buddy Bell was born in Pittsburgh. The son of former major league outfielder Gus Bell, Buddy would become a major leaguer himself in 1972—playing in 132 games with the Cleveland Indians.

August 28, 1945—Branch Rickey, general manager of the Brooklyn Dodgers, and Jackie Robinson, grandson of slaves, met for the first time. Their meeting set the ground work for Robinson to break major league baseball's color line.

August 29, 1965—Paul Waner died at the age of 62 in Sarasota, Florida. Paul Waner's rookie year with the Pittsburgh Pirates was 1926. He batted .336 and paced the National League in triples. In one game he stroked six hits using six different bats. In 1927, his brother Lloyd joined him and for fourteen years they formed a skillful combination in the Pirate lineup. Paul was 5'8½" and weighed 153 pounds. Lloyd was 5'9" and weighed 150 pounds. Paul was called "Big Poison." Lloyd was dubbed "Little Poison." Between them they collected 5,611 hits. Paul's lifetime average was .333 and in his twenty-year career, there were three batting titles. In 1952,

"Big Poison" was admitted to baseball's Hall of Fame.

August 29, 1971—Hank Aaron's 100th RBI of the 1971 season made him the first National League player to drive in 100 runs or more in eleven different seasons.

August 29, 1972—At the Olympics in Munich, Germany, Mark Spitz swam the 200-meter freestyle in the world record time of 1:52.78.

August 30, 1905—Ty Cobb appeared at the plate for his first major league at bat.

August 30, 1918—Ted Williams was born in San Diego, California. Dubbed the "Splendid Splinter," Williams was one of the top hitters in baseball history. He compiled a lifetime batting average of .344 and a slugging percentage of .634. Williams blasted 521 career home runs, scored nearly 1,800 runs and drove in over 1,800 runs. So keen was his batting eye that he walked over 2,000 times while striking out only 709 times. In 1941, he batted .406—the last time any player hit .400 or better. The handsome Red Sox slugger was the pride of all the fans that flocked to see him perform at Fenway Park.

August 30, 1945—The Boston Red Sox, the first major league team to travel by air, became the first major league baseball team to resume flying in airplanes after the lifting of war-time restrictions.

August 30, 1968—At Long Beach, California, Mark Spitz recorded a time of 55.6 seconds—a world's record for the 100-meter butterfly.

August 31, 1895—The first professional football game was played. Latrobe defeated Jeannette, 12–0 at Latrobe, Pennsylvania.

August 31, 1969—Rocky Marciano, former heavyweight champion of the world, was killed in a plane crash near Newton, Iowa.

SEPTEMBER

September 1, 1918—The major league baseball season came to an abrupt end because of the fighting in World War I.

September 1, 1924—Rocco Marchegiano was born in Brockton, Massachusetts. He would change his name to Rocky Marciano and reign as heavyweight boxing champion of the world from 1952 to 1956. He would win all of his 49 pro fights, 43 by KOs, eleven of them in the first round.

September 2, 1850—Alfred Goodwill Spalding was born. In 1876, he managed the Chicago White Stockings to the pennant and helped his own cause by winning 46 games as his team's top pitcher. In 1880 he retired as an active major leaguer and founded the sporting goods firm that made a fortune and made his name part of the language.

September 2, 1962—Ken Hubbs of the Chicago Cubs played in his 74th consecutive game without an error—a record for second basemen.

September 3, 1906—The longest fight ever staged under Queensberry Rules took place. Joe Gans fought "Battling" Nelson in a lightweight match at Goldfield, Nevada. Gans won in the 42nd round on a foul.

September 3, 1970—Vince Lombardi died at the age of 57. It was Lombardi who made the expression "winning isn't everything—it's the only thing" into his personal motto. In 1959, Lombardi took over as head coach of the Green Bay Packers. The year before the Packers had lost ten games tied one, and won one. By 1960, Lombardi steered Green Bay to the National Football League Western Division title. In 1961, Green Bay recorded its first World Championship in seventeen years. There was another championship in 1962, another in 1965, and another in 1966. Lombardi's Green Bay teams won the first two Super Bowls ever played. He symbolized a winner and the people of Green Bay and football fans lost a lot when he died.

September 3, 1973—Billie Jean King, citing the effects of the flu, defaulted to Julie Heldman. King's default was viewed as one of the most unusual twists of fate in the history of the United States Open tennis tournament.

September 4, 1953—The New York Yankees, managed by Casey Stengel, became the first team in baseball history to win five straight pennants.

September 5, 1906—Football's first legal forward pass was thrown. Brandbury Robinson of St. Louis University threw the pass which was caught by Jack Schneider in a game that took place at Waukesha, Wisconsin against Carroll College.

September 5, 1951—"Little Mo," Maureen Connolly, two days shy of her seventeenth birthday, won the United States amateur women singles tennis championship. She was the youngest winner of that event at that point in time.

September 5, 1960—Cassius Clay was the winner of the gold medal in the light heavyweight boxing division at the Olympics in Rome.

September 5, 1972—Eleven athletes—members of the Israeli Olympic Team—were murdered by Arab terrorists in Munich, Germany.

September 6, 1960—At the Rome Olympics, Australia's Herb Elliott ran the 1500-meter race in 3:56.6—a new world record.

September 7, 1928—Ray Benge of the Philadelphia Phillies pitched a 4–0 shutout over Boston even though he gave up eleven hits and three bases on balls.

September 8, 1950—Sandy Saddler knocked out Willie Pep to win the world featherweight boxing championship. Pep's shoulder was dislocated in the bout.

September 8, 1955—On their way to their first and only world championship, the Brooklyn Dodgers clinched the pennant on the earliest date in National League history.

September 8, 1973—On his way to becoming the all-time home run king, Hank Aaron pounded career homer number 709—a record for the most home runs hit by a player in one league.

September 9, 1908—Baseball's celebrated "bonehead play" took place. George Merkle was playing his first full game at first base for the New York Giants. It was his second season in the major leagues: the year before he had appeared in fifteen games. The Giants were in first place and the Cubs were challenging them. The two teams were tied, 1–1, in the bottom of the ninth inning. With two outs, the Giants' Moose McCormick was on third base and Merkle was on first. Al Bridwell slashed a single to centerfield. McCormick crossed the plate with what was apparently the winning run. Merkle, anxious to avoid the Polo Grounds crowd that surged out on the playing field, raced directly to the clubhouse instead of following through on the play and touching second base. Amid the confusion, Johnny Evers of the Cubs screamed for the baseball, obtained it somehow, stepped on second base, and claimed a force out on Merkle. When things calmed down, Umpire Hank O'Day agreed with Evers. The National League upheld O'Day, Evers and the Cubs. The run did not count; the game was not counted. Both teams played out their seasons and ended up tied for first place. The Cubs defeated the Giants in a replay of the game and Merkle is forever remembered for the "bonehead play" that cost the Giants the pennant.

September 9, 1954—It took Marilyn Bell twenty hours and fifty-six minutes to swim across Lake Ontario, but the effort made her the first person in history to ever accomplish that feat.

September 9, 1958—For the second year in a row, Althea Gibson was the victor in the United States Lawn Tennis singles championship for women.

September 9, 1960—Denver defeated Boston, 13–10, before 21,597 fans at Boston in the first American Football League regular season game.

September 9, 1965—Sandy Koufax's fourth no-hitter of his career was a perfect game. The Dodger Hall of Famer shut out the Cubs, 1–0.

September 10, 1929—Arnold Palmer, who would make golf history by becoming the first four-time winner of the Masters tournament, was born.

September 10, 1960—In one of the most stirring moments in the history of the Olympics, Abebe Bikila of Ethiopia, running barefooted, won the Marathon.

September 10, 1972—Amidst much controversy over the officiating, the first loss ever suffered by a United States basketball team took place in the Olympics. The Soviet Union eked out a 51–50 win in the game held at Munich, Germany.

September 10, 1972—Fabled Chicago Bear football player Gale Sayers retired.

September 10, 1973—Muhammad Ali was the victor in a heavyweight bout with Ken Norton. The win pleased Ali fans who had seen their favorite lose to Norton in March.

September 11, 1924—Dallas Cowboy coach Tom Landry was born.

September 11, 1942—Swedish track and field star Gunder Hagg capped an incredible string of running. He notched his eighth world record in 74 days.

September 11, 1946—The longest scoreless tie game in history was played at Ebbets Field. The game between the Dodgers and Cincinnati went nineteen innings.

September 11, 1951—By swimming the English Channel from England to France, Florence Chadwick became the first woman to swim the Channel in both directions. In 1950, Chadwick started her swim from France and wound up in England.

September 12, 1907—Hall of Famer Tris Speaker of the Boston Red Sox played the first of his 2,789 major league games over a 22-year career.

September 12, 1913—Jesse Owens was born. Twenty-three years later he would win four gold medals in track and field at the Berlin Olympics for the United States.

September 12, 1954—In Cleveland, 84,587 showed up for a doubleheader between the Yankees and Indians. It was a record mark for a regular season doubleheader.

September 12, 1964—The New York Jets played their first game in Shea Stadium before a then American Football League record crowd of 45,665.

September 13, 1849—The first death in an American boxing match took place. Chris Lilly kayoed Tom McCoy in a fight at Hastings, New York. McCoy died a short while after the fight.

September 13, 1923—George Burns of the Boston Red Sox performed the third unassisted triple play in history.

September 13, 1949—New York City was the site of the formation of the Ladies Professional Golf Association of America.

September 14, 1916—In his last pitching appearance, Christy Mathewson went out a winner notching his 373rd career victory. All of Mathewson's seventeen major league seasons were spent as a member of the New York Giants and all his wins were recorded as a member of that team except for his last one. Matty's 373rd triumph came as he pitched at the very tail end of his career for the Cincinnati Reds.

September 14, 1923—Jack Dempsey put down Luis Angel Firpo for the seventh and final time in their fight at the Polo Grounds in New York City. And Dempsey was declared the winner of the heavyweight battle in the 57th second of the second round.

September 14, 1924—Frank Chance, famed first baseman and manager, died in Los Angeles, California.

September 15, 1971—For the first time in sixteen years, Americans won both United States singles titles. Stan Smith and Billie Jean King were men's and women's singles champions in the U.S. Open tennis tournament.

September 15, 1974—In his first time at bat as a major league starter, Fred Lynn of the Red Sox hit a home run.

September 16, 1885—The Detroit Tigers purchased the entire Buffalo Bison franchise for $8,000. The real reason for the purchase was the obtaining of four players on the Buffalo roster known as the "Big Four." They were first baseman Dennis "Dan" Brouthers, third baseman James "Deacon" White, second baseman Harding Richardson and shortstop Jack Rowe. It was baseball's original mass player deal and an action that subsequently enabled Detroit to win its first pennant.

September 16, 1934—Elgin Baylor, who would become one of the greatest of forwards in the National Basketball Association, was born. Baylor played fourteen seasons for Minneapolis and Los Angeles and had a lifetime scoring average of 27.4 points a game.

September 16, 1953—The American League approved the transfer of the St. Louis Browns franchise to Baltimore.

September 16, 1960—Ninety-eight-year-old Amos Alonzo Stagg retired from football.

September 17, 1920—The first professional football player deal was transacted. Buffalo purchased Bob Nash from Akron for three hundred dollars.

September 17, 1941—In his first game as a St. Louis Cardinal, Stan Musial recorded two hits in a 3–2 Redbird victory. Twenty-two years later he would record two hits in another 3–2 Redbird victory and his last major league appearance.

September 17, 1954—An eighth round knockout of Ezzard Charles enabled Rocky Marciano to retain his heavyweight boxing title.

September 17, 1968—Gaylord Perry of the San Francisco Giants pitched a no-hitter against the St. Louis Cardinals; the next day Perry's Giants would be the victims of a no-hitter pitched by a Cardinal hurler.

September 18, 1908—Satchel Paige allegedly was born on this day. His draft card listed the date as documentation.

September 19, 1968—Ray Washburn of the St. Louis Cardinals pitched a 2–0, no-hitter against the San Francisco Giants. Washburn's no-hitter coupled with that of Gaylord Perry the day before produced the first back-to-back no-hitters in baseball history.

September 18, 1972—The National League's first black umpire—Art Williams—debuted in a game between the Padres and Los Angeles Dodgers in San Diego.

September 19, 1922—One of the great track and field stars in history—Emil Zatopek—was born. The Czech runner won gold medals four times in the 1948 and 1952 Olympics.

September 19, 1968—Denny McLain's 31st victory made him the first pitcher in the majors since 1931 to win that many games in one season.

September 20, 1917—Arnold "Red" Auerbach was born in Brooklyn, New York. He would go on to fame and accomplishment as a coach and a general manager for the Boston Celtics in the National Basketball Association.

September 20, 1948—The Mexican Baseball League, which had raided major league baseball signing some of its players, was forced to disband.

September 20, 1961—Playing in his 154th game of the 1961 season, Roger Maris of the New York Yankees blasted his 59th home run of the year. He went on to break Babe Ruth's record of 60 home runs in a season but not the Babe's record of 60 home runs in a 154-game season.

September 20, 1961—The Los Angeles Dodgers and the Chicago Cubs played to a thirteen inning, 3–3 tie in the last major league baseball game staged at the Los Angeles Coliseum.

September 20, 1973—In what was reported as the largest attendance for a single tennis match, 30,492 watched Billie Jean King defeat Bobby Riggs. The $100,000 "Battle of the Sexes" challenge match took place in the Houston Astrodome.

September 20, 1973—Willie Mays announced his retirement as a player would take place at the conclusion of the 1973 season.

September 21, 1902—Howie Morenz was born. In 1950, he would be awarded the title of the outstanding hockey player of the first half of the twentieth century by the press of Canada.

September 21, 1934—Dizzy Dean of the St. Louis Cardinals hurled a one-hitter against the Brooklyn Dodgers in the first game of a doubleheader. In the second game, his brother Paul no-hit the Dodgers. "If I'd a known that Paul was gonna do that," Diz said, "I'd a done the same."

September 21, 1948—French idol Marcel Cerdan won the middleweight boxing championship by knocking out Tony Zale.

September 21, 1955—A ninth round knockout of Archie Moore enabled Rocky Marciano to retain his undefeated hold on the heavyweight boxing title.

September 21, 1971—Permission was granted to the Washington Senators by American League club owners to move to Arlington, Texas for the start of the 1972 season.

September 22, 1927—More than 100,000 people paid $2,658,660 to witness a rematch of a heavyweight championship bout between Jack Dempsey and Gene Tunney. For the first six rounds, the battle at Soldier's Field, Chicago, was almost a repeat of the first encounter. Tunney kept piling up points. He scored repeatedly with his left hand. In the seventh round, Tunney was caught against the ropes by Dempsey. A solid left hook staggered Tunney. As the champion started to go down, Dempsey flailed away at him, landing several punishing shots. Tunney went down. It was the first time in his career that he had ever been knocked off his feet. Dempsey stood over the fallen champion anxious to finish him. Referee Dave Barry screamed to Dempsey to go to a neutral corner. Dempsey recalls: "I should have went back to the right corner but I didn't do it ... the referee grabbed me and shoved me and pushed me back. Then Tunney got up and won from then on out." Dempsey retired from boxing after that fight. What happened that night remains one of the most controversial topics in sports. Dempsey supporters claim the "long count" gave Tunney four extra seconds, for the referee delayed the count under the rules until Dempsey went to a neutral corner.

September 22, 1948—Batting against five different pitchers, Stan Musial of the St. Louis Cardinals stroked five hits.

September 22, 1959—For the first time in forty years, the Chicago White Sox won the American League pennant.

September 23, 1926—Gene Tunney defeated Jack Dempsey to become the new heavyweight champion of the world.

September 23, 1952—A thirteenth round knockout of Jersey Joe Walcott by Rocky Marciano made Marciano the new heavyweight champ of the world. It was the Brockton Blockbuster's 43rd straight win.

September 23, 1978—Lyman Bostick, who had been an outfielder with the Minnesota Twins and California Angels, died of shotgun wounds.

September 24, 1934—Babe Ruth appeared for the final time as a New York Yankee regular.

September 24, 1940—Hall of Famer Jimmie Foxx pounded his 500th career home run. He hit 34 more before he retired in 1945.

September 24, 1967—Jim Bakken kicked seven field goals for the St. Louis Cardinals to set a National Football League record.

September 25, 1882—Providence played Worcester as the first doubleheader in major league baseball took place.

September 25, 1926—Professional hockey franchises were granted to the Chicago Black Hawks and the Detroit Red Wings.

September 25, 1973—At Shea Stadium in New York City, more than 53,000 attended on Willie Mays Night—the final appearance of the "Say Hey Kid" as a player.

September 26, 1908—Ed Reulbach of the Chicago Cubs pitched a doubleheader shutout against the Dodgers. He won the first game, 5–0, allowing five hits and came back to win the second game, 3–0, with a three-hitter.

September 26, 1947—The joint sponsors for the first World Series in history to be televised were chosen: Gillette and Ford. Baseball Commissioner Happy Chandler turned down a bid by a brewery company to sponsor the series.

September 26, 1961—Roger Maris pounded his 60th home run to tie Babe Ruth's season record.

September 27, 1923—New York Yankee slugger and Hall of Famer Lou Gehrig recorded the first of his 493 major league home runs. The homer was hit off Boston Red Sox pitcher Bill Piercy at Fenway Park.

September 27, 1950—Ezzard Charles defeated Joe Louis to hold on to the world heavyweight boxing championship. It was only the second defeat in 62 bouts for Louis.

September 27, 1956—Mildred (Babe) Didrickson Zaharias, one of the greatest women athletes in American history, died.

September 27, 1964—Houston played its last game in Colt Stadium and defeated Los Angeles, 1–0, in twelve innings.

September 28, 1920—The eight Chicago White Sox players who allegedly "threw" the 1919 World Series, were indicted by a grand jury in Chicago.

September 28, 1935—Bruce Crampton was born. In 1962–63, Crampton would be dubbed "Iron Man" for his performance in 38 straight golf events during the tour season.

September 28, 1941—On the final day of the season, Ted Williams of the Boston Red Sox stroked six hits in six times at bat to clinch a .400 batting average for the year.

September 28, 1960—In his last major league game and last time at bat, Ted Williams pounded a home run. It was the 521st home run of the "Splendid Splinter's" career.

September 29, 1768—A twelve shilling fee was paid to a jockey by George Washington to race his pacer near Mt. Vernon.

September 29, 1880—Baseball's first professional game was played. The Metropolitans of Manhattan defeated the Washington Nationals, 4–2, in a five inning contest at the Polo Grounds, then located at Sixth Avenue and 110th Street in Manhattan.

September 29, 1946—The St. Louis Cardinals and the Brooklyn Dodgers finished the National League season with identical records and tied for first place. The first National League playoff in history took place as a result. The Cardinals won two of three games and the National League pennant.

September 29, 1951—Football's first TV network color transmission took place. CBS televised the University of California's 35–0 triumph over the University of Pennsylvania from Philadelphia's Franklin Field.

September 29, 1954—Willie Mays of the New York Giants executed one of the most dramatic plays in World Series history. Vic Wertz of Cleveland blasted a pitch by Don Liddle to the distant reaches of centerfield. Mays took off the instant his instincts told him where the ball was headed. Back, back, back, he raced toward the bleacher wall. The ball was dropping and Mays was still running. Approaching the running track—his number 24 lined up almost with home plate—

Mays stretched out his arms as the ball went over his shoulder. On the warning track, 460 feet from home plate he whirled, twisted toward the plate, and fired the ball back to the infield. The Indians did not score that inning. The Giants went on to win the game and the World Series and many claimed the catch by Mays took the momentum away from Cleveland.

September 29, 1957—The Giants of New York and the Dodgers of Brooklyn played their last games. Just 11,606 attended the final game in the Polo Grounds. The Giants lost to the Pirates, 9–1. The Dodgers defeated the Phillies, 2–1, at Philadelphia in the last game the Brooklyn team ever played. Less than 10,000 fans attended the contest that lasted just one hour and 58 minutes.

September 29, 1963—In his 22nd and final year as a major leaguer, in his 10,972nd and final time at bat, St. Louis Cardinal star Stan Musial recorded his 3,630th hit and 1,950th run batted in.

September 30, 1916—The New York Giants had their winning streak of twenty-six games—the longest in modern baseball history—stopped. The loss came in the second game of a double-header as the Braves defeated the Giants, 8–3.

September 30, 1927—Babe Ruth smashed his 60th home run of the season—a record-setting clout.

September 20, 1972—Roberto Clemente of the Pittsburgh Pirates recorded the 3,000th and final hit of his life. Clemente said of the historic hit: "I give this hit to the fans of Pittsburgh and to the people of Puerto Rico."

September 30, 1973—Hank Aaron played his final game of the season but was unsuccessful in attempting to hit a home run. Aaron ended the year with a career total of 713 homers, one shy of Babe Ruth's all-time record.

September 30, 1973—The New York Yankees completed their 50th anniversary season at the Stadium. On this day Ralph Houk resigned as manager of the Yankees.

OCTOBER

October 1, 1903—The Pittsburgh Pirates, winners of their third straight pennant, faced the Boston Red Sox in the first game of the first modern World Series in baseball history. Deacon Phillippe of Pittsburgh bested Boston's Cy Young, 7–3. The first World Series home run was hit by Pirate outfielder Jim Sebring, who had four RBI's in the game. Phillippe struck out ten batters and went on to be a winner in three of the first four games in the series—but the Red Sox won the title, five games to three.

October 1, 1932—It was the third game of the World Series between the New York Yankees and the Chicago Cubs. The Yankees had won the first two games in New York City and were now in Chicago and confident of wrapping up the series. Babe Ruth had homered for the Yanks with two men on in the first inning. In the fifth inning he came to bat again. Chicago fans had taunted and teased him. They had thrown assorted projectiles at Ruth from the stands. Ruth came up to the plate. The score was tied, 4–4. There was one out. Charlie Root, the Cub pitcher, got a strike past Ruth. Chicago fans and players renewed their razzing of the Babe who held up one finger to indicate—strike one. The next pitch was a ball. The next pitch was a called strike two. Cub players screamed at Ruth from their dugout, and he held up two fingers—shaking his big hand at the Cub players. He glowered at the Cubs in their dugout and then pointed to the flagpole to the right of the scoreboard in centerfield. It was a promise of what he intended to do with the next pitch. And he did it. Ruth smashed the ball out to deep centerfield—it cleared the park and smashed into an office building. It was the longest homer ever hit in the ballpark of the Chicago Cubs. Ruth ran the bases, trotting out what would be known as "the called shot," and he accentuated what he had done by making uncomplimentary gestures to the Cub players and their fans. There are many who claim that home run was the most dramatic achievement of Ruth's most dramatic career.

October 1, 1945—Rod Carew, who would become one of baseball's top hitters, was born in Gatun, Panama.

October 1, 1949—They called Tommy Henrich "Old Reliable" and he proved it on this day once again. The Brooklyn Dodgers and Henrich's Yankees were scoreless after eight innings of the first game of the 1949 World Series. Don Newcombe of the Dodgers was matching Allie Reynolds of the Yankees—almost pitch for pitch. Henrich led off the bottom of the ninth inning and homered to give the Yankees a 1–0 victory. "It's a good thing Henrich did that," said Reynolds, "we could have been pitching that way for a week."

October 1, 1950—The Philadelphia Phillies won their first pennant since 1913. Dick Sisler's home run in the last game of the season defeated the Brooklyn Dodgers.

October 1, 1961—On the final day of the season, New York Yankee slugger Roger Maris stroked the ball 360 feet into the lower deck in right field at Yankee Stadium. The blow was the 61st home run of the 1961 season for Maris—breaking the record of 60 set by Babe Ruth. "If I never hit another home run," Maris said afterward, "this is the one they can never take away from me."

October 1, 1977—Pele retired as an active participant in the game of soccer, after what he termed his "mission" of giving the sport momentum was concluded.

October 2, 1936—The "Murderer's Row" of the New York Yankees operated at peak efficiency in the second game of the World Series. The Bronx Bombers scored an 18–4 victory over the New York Giants. Each player in the Yankee lineup recorded at least one hit and scored at least one run. Bill Dickey and Tony Lazerri each drove in five runs. Lazerri pounded a grand slam home run; Dickey hit a three-run homer.

October 2, 1949—The Yankees defeated the Red Sox and the Dodgers defeated the Cardinals on the last day of the baseball season. It was the first time in forty-one years that the pennant races in both the National League and American League were decided on the final day of the season.

October 2, 1954—The New York Giants defeated the Cleveland Indians, 7–4, to win the World Series. It was the first World Series win for the Giants since 1946. The victory gave the Giants a sweep of the four-game series—a competition in which they pounded the highly regarded Indian pitching staff for twenty-one runs. Cleveland hurlers had gone through the entire 1954 season with a combined earned run average of 2.78.

October 2, 1968—"It was the greatest pitching performance I've ever seen." That was the statement made by Detroit manager Mayo Smith after Bob Gibson struck out a record seventeen Tigers, allowed but five hits, and powered his St. Louis team to a 4–0 World Series game victory.

October 2, 1973—Paavo Nurmi died. The "Phantom Finn" had won six individual track and field Olympic gold medals and set twenty-five world records.

October 3, 1947—The fourth game of the 1947 World Series is remembered by many baseball people. The game had a special meaning for Yankee pitcher Bill Bevens and Dodger pinch-hitter Cookie Lavagetto. Bevens allowed only one hit in the game—a two-out, pinch-hit double to Lavagetto—the last man to bat as the Dodgers won, 3–2.

October 3, 1951—At 3:58 P.M. in the Polo Grounds in New York City, in the last game and last inning of the National League playoffs, Bobby Thomson pounded a one-strike fastball thrown by Ralph Branca. The ball streaked in a low and curving line and landed 315 feet away from home plate in the stands. The Polo Grounds became a place of pandemonium. New York Giant radio announcer Russ Hodges screamed out eight times: "The Giants win the pennant! The Giants win the pennant!" It was one of baseball's most memorable moments because not only had the Giants come from 13 ½ games back in mid-August, they had beaten their main rivals, the great Brooklyn Dodgers.

October 3, 1951—Dave Sands was the victor over Bobo Olson in their middleweight bout—the first fight televised coast to coast.

October 3, 1971—A victory in a tennis tournament at Phoenix Arizona made Billie Jean King the first woman athlete to record $100,000 in earnings in a single year.

October 4, 1948—The Cleveland Indians defeated the Boston Red Sox, 8–3, in the first American League playoff game ever. Indian player-manager Lou Boudreau helped his own cause with four hits.

October 4, 1955—The Dodgers of Brooklyn defeated the New York Yankees, 2–0, in the final game of the 1955 World Series. The triumph provided the Brooklyn Dodgers with their first and only world championship ever.

October 4, 1975—May Bundy died. In 1905, she became the first American to win a tennis title at Wimbledon.

October 5, 1941—The Brooklyn Dodgers faced the New York Yankees in the fourth game of the World Series. The Dodgers had never won a world championship but were ahead two games to one and were leading 4–3 in the top of the ninth with two men out. Dodger relief pitcher Hugh Casey got two strikes on Tommy Henrich. The next pitch was in on Henrich and down. The Yankee outfielder swung and missed. Somehow the pitch got away from Dodger catcher Mickey Owen and Henrich reached first base. The Yankees took advantage of the lapse by Owens— scoring four times for a 7–4 victory. The big blow for the Yankees was a double by Charlie Keller that scored two runs.

October 5, 1942—The New York Yankees lost their first World Series in sixteen years. The Cardinals defeated the Bronx Bombers for their fourth straight win and the world championship.

October 5, 1947—The last game ever played by utility outfielder Al Gionfriddo provided baseball with one of its unforgettable moments. The Brooklyn Dodgers led the New York Yankees, 8–5, in the bottom of the sixth inning of the sixth game of the 1947 World Series. With two men on base, Joe DiMaggio drove the ball into deep left field. Gionfriddo raced after the ball. He gloved it just as it was about to go over the 415-marker into the left field bullpen. The Yankees lost the game, 8–6, but won the World Series the next day. Dodger fans still remember Gionfriddo's spectacular catch.

October 5, 1953—A victory over the Dodgers gave the New York Yankees and manager Casey Stengel their fifth straight World Series win. The feat was a record for a team and a manager up to that point in time.

October 6, 1824—This was the birth date of Henry Chadwick who would invent the scorer's system and the rule book that would become integral parts of baseball record-keeping.

October 6, 1923—Ernie Padgett of the Boston Braves recorded the fourth unassisted triple play in major league baseball history.

October 6, 1977—The first match in history took place between the United States soccer team and a club that represented the People's Republic of China.

October 7, 1947—Jack Kramer announced that he would become a tennis pro.

October 7, 1965—Robert Mitera achieved the longest hole-in-one at the tenth hole at the Miracle Hills Golf Club, Omaha, Nebraska. A fifty-mile-an-hour gust carried the ball over a 290-yard drop-off for the record 444-yard hole-in-one.

October 8, 1939—Andy Uram of Green Bay ran 97 yards from scrimmage against the Cardinals to set a National Football League record.

October 8, 1950—The fourth National Hockey League All-Star game was staged. Detroit triumphed, 8–1, and stopped an All-Star three-year winning streak. Left wing Ted Lindsay scored three goals to pace the Red Wings.

October 8, 1956—Don Larsen's "perfect" pitching gave the New York Yankees a 2–0 triumph in the World Series over the Brooklyn Dodgers. Larsen faced 27 batters—none of whom reached base against him.

October 8, 1961—Whitey Ford of the New York Yankees was forced to leave game four of the 1961 World Series because of an ankle injury. Ford left after extending his streak of scoreless innings pitched in the World Series to 32—breaking Babe Ruth's record of 29 2/3 innings. Jim Coates pitched the last four innings for the Yankees who defeated the Reds, 7–0.

October 8, 1978—Jim "Junior" Gilliam died. He was a favorite of Brooklyn Dodger fans when he played the infield for the team in the 1950's.

October 9, 1915—President Woodrow Wilson became the first American Chief Executive to attend a World Series game. Wilson appeared for the second game of the 1915 World Series between the Philadelphia Phillies and Boston Red Sox.

October 9, 1949—Baseball's first "night" World Series game was played. The game was between the Yankees and Dodgers at Ebbets Field. The lights were turned on in the final innings of the contest.

October 9, 1960—Howard Glenn of the New York Titans died as a result of being injured in a game against the Houston Oilers.

October 9, 1966—A Frank Robinson home run in the fourth inning gave the Baltimore Orioles a 1–0 victory over the Los Angeles Dodgers and a sweep of all four games in the World Series. Jim Palmer, Wally Bunker and Dave McNally each pitched a shutout against the Dodgers in the last three games. McNally's four-hit effort in the fourth game capped a streak of 33 straight scoreless innings pitched by Baltimore hurlers in the series.

October 10, 1920—One of baseball's strangest and most memorable games was played. The Cleveland Indians defeated Brooklyn, 8–1, in game five of the World Series which saw Elmer Smith hit the first bases loaded homer in the World Series and Wambsganss perform an unassisted triple play.

October 10, 1951—Joe DiMaggio played his last baseball game. DiMag once again played for a winner as the Yankees defeated the New York Giants, 4–3, in the sixth game of the World Series. It was the Yankee Clipper's 51st World Series appearance—a record.

October 10, 1957—Yogi Berra appeared in his 53rd World Series game to break a record set by

Joe DiMaggio. Berra's record breaking appearance was in the final game of the World Series between the Yankees and the Braves of Milwaukee.

October 10, 1957—The Milwaukee Braves defeated the Yankees in the final game of the World Series leaving New York City without a baseball world champion for the first time since 1949.

October 10, 1961—Two new National League teams, the New York Mets and the Houston Colts, bought talent made available in the expansion team purchase. The Mets acquired twenty-two players for $1,800,000. The Colts obtained twenty-three athletes for $1,850,000.

October 10, 1962—The first Olympic Games staged in Asia began. Athletes from nations of the world assembled for the XVIII Summer Olympic Games in Tokyo, Japan.

October 11, 1913—Eddie Plank faced only twenty-nine men and allowed two scattered singles as he pitched his Philadelphia teammates to a 2–1 victory over the New York Giants enabling Philadelphia to win the World Series.

October 11, 1951—National Football League Commissioner Bert Bell suffered a heart attack during the final two minutes of a game at Philadelphia between the Eagles and Pittsburgh Steelers. Bell died as a result of the heart attack.

October 12, 1920—Man o' War won his last race —a match, competition against Sir Barton at Kenilworth Park in Canada. The victory purse made Man o' War the biggest thoroughbred money winner at that point in time.

October 12, 1923—A Casey Stengel home run gave the Giants a 1-0 win over the Yankees in a World Series game. The crowd of 62,817 was the largest attendance at a baseball game to that date.

October 12, 1929—The Philadelphia Athletics scored ten times in the seventh inning to win the fourth game of the World Series against the Chicago Cubs. Hack Wilson of the Cubs aided the Philadelphia cause by losing two balls in the sun.

October 12, 1968—Norma Enriquetta Basilo Satelo, became the first woman in modern times to light an Olympic Torch. She opened the first Olympics held in Latin America as the games got underway at Mexico City.

October 13, 1903—Boston defeated Pittsburgh, 3-0, to win the first modern World Series.

October 13, 1926—Eddie Yost was born. He would play major league baseball for nearly two decades and would earn the nickname "the walking man." His 1614 walks—almost a base on balls a game placed Yost fifth on the all-time list.

October 13, 1931—Eddie Mathews was born in Texarkana, Texas. His seventeen-year career as a major league ballplayer gave him the distinction of being one of the few to perform for the Boston Braves, Milwaukee Braves and Atlanta Braves.

October 13, 1947—The first National Hockey League All-Star game was played. The All-Stars defeated the Toronto Maple Leafs, 4–3.

October 14, 1914—Harry Brecheen, who in 1946 would become the first southpaw pitcher to win three games in a World Series, was born.

October 14, 1973—Jackie Stewart, a three-time world champion driver, retired from auto racing.

October 15, 1945—Jim Palmer was born in New York City. He joined the Baltimore Orioles in 1965 and began an illustrious pitching career.

October 16, 1910—At Conway, Missouri, Stanley Ketchel, the world middleweight boxing champ, was shot and killed.

October 16, 1969—A fifth game 5–3 win over the Baltimore Orioles made the New York Mets world champions. The "Amazing Mets" had started the 1969 season as 100–1 underdogs to win the World Series.

October 17, 1848—Candy Cummings was born. Cummings would be credited in 1864 with the invention of baseball's curve ball and would become a member of the Hall of Fame.

October 17, 1883—A standardized numerical scoring system was adopted for football. Five points were awarded for a field goal, two points for a touchdown, a point for a safety and four points for a goal on an attempt to score after a touchdown.

October 17, 1938—This was the birth date of the man destined to become one of the world's greatest stunt daredevils—Evel Knievel.

October 17, 1946—Robert Seagren, who would gain fame as a pole vaulter, was born.

October 17, 1977—Cal Hubbard died. A football tackle and a baseball umpire—he was the only person ever elected to both the football and baseball Hall of Fame.

October 18, 1924—Red Grange scored four touchdowns on long runs in the first ten minutes of a game to lead his Illinois team to a 39–14 defeat of Michigan.

October 18, 1924—Notre Dame scored a 13–7 win over Army. That game and the performance of the "Fighting Irish" backfield inspired Grantland Rice to write his "Four Horseman" article in the *New York Herald Tribune* that immortalized the players.

October 18, 1950—Connie Mack retired from baseball after sixty-seven years in the game. He was a major league manager for fifty-three years.

He ranks first in games managed, games won and games lost.

October 18, 1960—The New York Yankees fired Casey Stengel as manager. The field leader of the team since 1949, Stengel was dismissed according to the Yankees because he had reached their organization's mandatory retirement age.

October 18, 1969—Lew Alcindor (Kareem Abdul-Jabbar) played in his first professional basketball game. A national TV sports audience and 7,782 in Milwaukee watched the historic debut of the UCLA three-time All-American. Milwaukee won the game, 119–110. Their touted rookie scored 29 points, collected a dozen rebounds, notched six assists, three assists and three blocked shots.

October 19, 1876—Mordecai Centennial Brown was born. His middle name came as a result of the year in which he was born—America's centennial. His nickname "Three-Finger" derived from a childhood accident that mangled his right hand and made him lose two fingers. It was also, according to Brown, the reason for his baseball success with the Chicago Cubs and other teams he pitched for. "It gave me a bigger dip for my pitches," he said. Brown's dip enabled him to record a lifetime earned run average of 2.06, the third best in baseball history and more than good enough to get him admitted to the Hall of Fame in 1949.

October 20, 1931—Mickey Mantle was born in Commerce, Oklahoma. Two decades later he became a member of the New York Yankees. For eighteen seasons, Mantle was a fixture in center-field for the Yankees. Four times he led the American League in home runs. He was a rare blend of raw power and track star speed.

October 20, 1965—Detroit's Gordie Howe broke the career All-Star game career goal record by scoring his eighth and ninth to lead the All-Stars to a 5–2 triumph over the Canadiens.

October 20, 1973—On a day that President Nixon signed into law a bill authorizing a national medal to commemorate Jim Thorpe, one of America's greatest athletes, Notre Dame crushed Army in a game that accentuated one of America's great collegiate football rivalries. The total points scored were the most ever recorded in a game between the traditional rivals.

October 21, 1928—Whitey Ford was born in New York City. A star southpaw for the New York Yankees for sixteen seasons, Ford won 236 games, lost just 106 and notched an ERA of 2.75. His .690 winning percentage places him second on the all-time list.

October 21, 1980—The Philadelphia Phillies edged the Kansas City Royals, 4–1, in the sixth game of the World Series to win the Fall Classic for the first time in their 98-year history. The Phillies took the lead in the game in the sixth inning and never lost it. A crowd of 65,838 at Veterans Stadium provided a roaring backdrop for the victory. Tug McGraw saved the game for Philadelphia starter Steve Carlton.

October 22, 1907—Jimmy Foxx was born. His slugging ability earned him a place in baseball's Hall of Fame.

October 22, 1939—The first professional football game ever televised came from Ebbets Field. It was a Brooklyn Dodger 23–14 victory over the Philadelphia Eagles.

October 22, 1950—A 70–27 slaughter of the Baltimore Colts by the Los Angeles Rams enabled the two teams to set a National Football League record for most points scored in a regular season game.

October 22, 1972—The A's edged Cincinnati, 3–2, in the seventh game of the World Series to become World Champions. It was the first World Series triumph for the A's franchise since 1930—a time when the team was located in Philadelphia. Catcher Gene Tenace collected two runs batted in, a single and a double, to pace the A's attack.

October 22, 1974—The New York Yankees traded outfielder Bobby Murcer to the San Francisco Giants for Bobby Bonds.

October 23, 1940—Edson Arantes De Nascimento, who would best be known as Pele, was born in Tres Coracoes, Brazil. As a poor youth he learned to kick a "soccer ball" that was actually an old stuffed sock. Years later, after scoring his 1,000th goal, he was awarded a four-

pound soccer ball made of gold. The only soccer
player to have performed on three World Championship soccer teams, Pele scored more goals
than any other player in soccer history.

October 23, 1945—Branch Rickey signed Jackie
Robinson to a contract to play the 1946 season
for the Montreal Royals—the top farm team of
the Brooklyn Dodgers. The signing set the stage
for Robinson to break major league baseball's
color line in 1947.

October 23, 1968—Kenya's Kip Keino was the
1500-meter gold medal winner in the Olympics.

October 23, 1978—Bryan Trottier of the New
York Islanders broke a National Hockey League
record by scoring six points in one period.

October 24, 1857—The Sheffield Football Club
of England was formed. It is today the world's
oldest football (soccer) club.

October 24, 1926—One of pro football's most
outstanding quarterbacks was born—Y.
(Yelberton) A. (Abraham) Tittle.

October 24, 1972—Jackie Robinson died. He
was fifty-three years old and had lost the sight in
one eye.

October 25, 1869—This was the birth date of
John Heisman, the man who lent his name to the
trophy symbolic of the top collegiate football

player. A football coach from 1892-1928, Heisman invented the spinner play and the direct snap from center.

October 25, 1923—Bobby Thomson was born in Glasgow, Scotland. In 1946, he became a member of the New York Giants. A major league baseball player for fifteen years, Thomson stroked 264 home runs but will forever be remembered for the one hit on an October day in 1951. It came in the final inning of the final game of the 1951 National League playoff and rocketed the Giants to victory over the Dodgers. Dubbed "the shot heard 'round the world," Thomson's home run gave the Giants the pennant and sent all of Brooklyn into despair.

October 25, 1973—In Addis Ababa, Ethiopia, Abebe Bikila died of a brain hemorrhage after suffering a stroke. He was 46 years old. He left three sons, a daughter and a wife. He had been paralyzed from the waist down for 4 ½ years following an automobile accident. He was the only man in history to win two Olympic marathons. In 1960, all the racing shoes he tried hurt his feet as he got ready for the Olympics. On smooth roads he felt that he was faster and more comfortable running without shoes. "I will win without shoes," he said. "I will make some history for Africa." He ran barefooted through the Rome night and set a new Olympic and world record time of 2:15:16.2. In 1964, in Tokyo, Bikila wore shoes. He was even more of a force than in Rome. He won easily—the second place finisher was more than four minutes behind him. In 1969, the tragic car accident confined him to a wheelchair. It was a sad sight for all those who loved athletics to see Bikila a victim of cruel fate.

October 26, 1863—Freeman's Tavern in London was the scene for a conference among British sports people that today is viewed as the occasion of the birth of soccer. That date saw the formation of the Football Association (F.A.)—an organization devoted exclusively to the kicking game of football, as distinct from rugby.

October 26, 1951—At Madison Square Garden in New York City, former heavyweight champion of the world Joe Louis was defeated by Rocky Marciano.

October 26, 1980—The New York Marathon was won by Alberto Salazar, a native of Cuba. A record 14,012 starters competed in the 11th running of the New York City event. Bill Rodgers, who had won the last four NYC marathons, finished in fifth place.

October 27, 1922—Ralph Kiner was born in Santa Rita, New Mexico. He would pound 369 career home runs and lead the National League in homers for seven straight years.

October 27, 1949—Marcel Cerdan died in an airplane crash in the Azores. He was on the plane preparing to return to the United States to fight Jake La Motta and reclaim the middleweight boxing championship of the world. Cerdan had defeated Tony Zale for the championship but held it for just nine months. He lost it to La Motta, unable to continue fighting past the tenth round due to a shoulder injury. A handsome Frenchman, Cerdan's love affair with French singer Edith Piaf earned him fame outside the boxing ring.

October 27, 1980—Ralph Houk, age 61, was named manager of the Boston Red Sox. "I'd like to win one more pennant," said Houk, who had been out of baseball for the past two years after being manager of the Detroit Tigers for five years.

October 28, 1937—Lenny Wilkens, who would star in the NBA and become an outstanding coach for the Seattle Supersonics, was born in Brooklyn, New York.

October 28, 1961—At Flushing Meadow Park in Queens, New York, ground was broken for the building of a municipal stadium. It would be called Shea Stadium—in honor of the man who brought National League baseball back to New York. It would become the future home of the New York Mets and the New York Jets.

October 28, 1973—Secretariat won his final race by 6½ lengths, the Canadian International Stakes at Toronto's Woodbine.

October 28, 1975—Georges Carpentier died. His greatest fame came as a result of the first million dollar gate in history when he lost in 1921 on a fourth round knockout to Jack Dempsey.

October 29, 1948—Sandy Saddler scored an upset knockout victory over Willie Pep and was crowned world featherweight boxing champ.

October 29, 1973—O.J. Simpson became the first player in National Football League history to gain more than a thousand yards in seven games.

October 30, 1973—Tom Seaver of the New York Mets was voted the Cy Young Award. He thus became the first pitcher in history to win the award with less than twenty victories.

October 30, 1974—Muhammad Ali regained his heavyweight crown by knocking out George Foreman in their title match held in Zaire.

October 31, 1947—Frank Shorter was born. In 1972, he won the gold medal in the Olympic marathon and became the first American in sixty-four years to win the event.

NOVEMBER

November 1, 1872—England played soccer against Scotland in the first international match in history. The final score was 0-0, a goalless draw.

November 1, 1924—The Boston Bruins were given a franchise and admitted to the National Hockey League. They became the first American team to compete in the NHL.

November 1, 1947—On this date, Man o' War, one of the great race horses in history, died.

November 1, 1950—Chuck Cooper, the first black player drafted by the National Basketball Association, played his first game for the Boston Celtics against the Pistons in a game at Fort Wayne, Indiana.

November 2, 1938—Babe Ruth, released after the 1938 season as a coach for the Brooklyn Dodgers, applied for the position as manager of the St. Louis Browns.

November 3, 1918—Bob Feller, who would pitch three no-hit games for the Cleveland Indians and be admitted to baseball's Hall of Fame, was born.

November 4, 1884—The longest run in football history was recorded on this day—a record that will never be broken. The run was 115 yards—performed by Yale's Wyllys Terry in a game against Wesleyan. Terry grabbed a pass from center while positioned in punt formation, five yards behind his own goal line and then ran the entire length of the then 110-yard gridiron. After Terry's run, football officials decided that no player would ever again be credited with a run of more than 100 yards, no matter how many yards he ran.

November 4, 1950—Grover Cleveland Alexander died in St. Paul, Nebraska. A pitching great, he was admitted in 1938 to the Hall of Fame.

November 4, 1959—Ernie Banks of the Chicago Cubs was voted the Most Valuable Player award by the Baseball Writers Association.

November 5, 1970—Charlie Root died. He was the Chicago Cub pitcher in the 1932 World Series who threw the pitch that Babe Ruth signalled he would hit for a home run. Ruth made good on his promise.

November 5, 1971—The Los Angeles Lakers began a streak of 33 straight wins—the longest in National Basketball Association history.

November 6, 1861—This was the birth date of James Naismith, the man who invented the sport of basketball.

November 6, 1869—The first collegiate football game in the United States was held at New Brunswick, New Jersey. Rutgers defeated Princeton, 6-4. Twenty-five players were on each team.

November 6, 1887—Walter Johnson was born. He struck out 3,497—more than any other pitcher in major league history.

November 6, 1961—The United States Post Office issued a commemorative stamp for the 100th anniversary of the birth of James Naismith, the man who invented basketball.

November 6, 1969—The first tie vote in the history of the Cy Young Award took place. Detroit's Denny McLain and Baltimore's Mike Cuellar received the same amount of votes in the contest to determine the American League's best pitcher.

November 7, 1938—Jim Kaat was born in Zeeland, Michigan. In 1959, he became a pitcher for the Washington Senators. In 1980, he began his 22nd season as a major league pitcher—filling a role as a spot starter and reliever for the St. Louis Cardinals. Kaat thus became one of the few players in major league history to play ball in four different decades.

November 7, 1963—Yankee catcher Elston Howard became the first black player in the

American League to win the Most Valuable Player award.

November 7, 1973—A state civil rights hearing decision made New Jersey the first state to mandate that girls had the right to play together with boys on Little League teams.

November 7, 1978—Gene Tunney died. He defeated Jack Dempsey and reigned as heavyweight champion of the world from 1926 to 1928.

November 8, 1954—The transfer of the Philadelphia Athletics baseball franchise to Kansas City, Missouri, was approved by American League owners.

November 8, 1970—New Orleans Saints kicker Tom Dempsey recorded a sixty-three yard field goal. The record kick enabled the Saints to defeat the Detroit Lions, 19-17. Dempsey was born with only half a right foot and no right hand.

November 8, 1971—The National Hockey League announced the granting of franchises to Long Island and Atlanta. The two new clubs, the Islanders and the Flames, began play in the 1972-73 season.

November 9, 1912—Jim Thorpe recorded perhaps his greatest day in his entire football career, leading his Carlisle team to a 27-6 victory over Army. Twenty-two of Carlisle's points were scored by Thorpe, including six that came on a 95-yard run.

November 9, 1946—Army and Navy played a scoreless tie game. Their football contest had been so attractive to football fans that more than a million ticket requests had to be denied.

November 9, 1952—The 325th goal of Maurice Richard's career—a record to that point in time was scored by the Montreal star. The puck was given to England's Queen Elizabeth.

November 9, 1961—A proviso that restricted membership in the Professional Golfers' Association to caucasians only was removed from that organization's constitution.

November 10, 1953—Larry Christenson was born in Everett, Washington. Twenty years later he appeared in his first major league game as a pitcher for the Philadelphia Phillies.

November 11, 1868—America's first amateur track meet was held. It was sponsored by the New York Athletic Club.

November 11, 1951—Bob Mathias, the Olympic decathlon gold medal winner ran a kickoff back ninety-six yards. His score was the margin of victory as Stanford defeated the University of California, 27-20.

November 11, 1955—It was announced by the International Olympic Committee that officials for the 1956 games would be required to take an impartiality oath. The reason behind the announcement was the feeling that too nationalistic a spirit had influenced the judging in some of the previous Olympics.

November 12, 1920—Kenesaw Mountain Lindis was elected baseball's first commissioner.

November 12, 1927—Green jerseys and stockings became part of the Notre Dame football team's uniform for the first time as ND played Army in NY. The team had worn blue jerseys since 1887.

November 12, 1931—The Toronto Maple Leafs' new arena, Maple Leaf Gardens, opened for competition.

November 12, 1944—Army defeated Notre Dame, 59-0, for the first win in the historic rivalry since 1931. Army's team was led by Glenn Davis and Doc Blanchard.

November 12, 1955—The first three inductees to the Jockey Hall of Fame at Pimlico, Maryland, were Eddie Arcaro, Earle Sande, and George Woolf.

November 13, 1941—It was announced that Joe Louis would fight Buddy Baer in New York on January 9, 1942 for the benefit of the Navy Relief Fund.

November 14, 1943—Sid Luckman threw seven touchdown passes. The Chicago Bear quarterback became the first player to ever accomplish that feat.

November 14, 1970—Thirty-five members of the Marshall University football team died in a plane crash near Kenova, West Virginia.

November 15, 1939—The New York Giants announced that for the 1940 season a 200-million candlepower lighting system would be installed at the Polo Grounds.

November 15, 1950—Arthur Dorrington became organized hockey's first black player. Dorrington signed an Eastern League contract with Atlantic City.

November 15, 1954—Twenty-seven-year-old Gallant Fox died. The great race horse had won the Kentucky Derby, the Belmont and the Preakness in 1930.

November 15, 1973—A three goal, four assist effort by Bobby Orr led the Boston Bruins to a 10–2 romp over the New York Rangers.

November 16, 1938—Willie Hall of England's Tottenham Hotspur scored three goals in 3 ½ minutes. It was the most goals in the shortest period of time ever scored in an international match.

November 16, 1957—Oklahoma fans were disappointed as its team lost, 7–0 to Notre Dame. The game was tied in with Oklahoma's celebration of its fiftieth year of statehood.

November 16, 1972—For the first time in National Basketball Association history, a team lost its first round draft pick for violating league rules. The Seattle Supersonics were declared in violation of NBA rules by signing John Brisker of the American Basketball Association.

November 17, 1944—Tom Seaver was born in Fresno, California. Twenty-three years later, he began his pitching career with the New York Mets.

November 17, 1954—Jimmy Carter recorded a technical knockout over Paddy DeMarco in their bout in San Francisco to become world light-weight champion for the third time.

November 17, 1959—Willie McCovey, who would play in the National League through four decades, was named Rookie of the Year.

November 17, 1968—What would become known as "the Heidi event" took place. NBC was televising a football game between the New York Jets and the Oakland Raiders. The network did not televise the last minute of the game, choosing instead to transmit a production of *Heidi*, a children's program. Oakland scored twice in nine seconds to win 43–32. Thousands of football fans all over the United States protested the NBC decision.

November 18, 1922—Marjorie Gestring was born. In 1936 she became the youngest woman at the point in time to win a gold medal in the Olympics. Ms. Gestring was the victor in the women's springboard diving event.

November 18, 1954—The New York Yankees and the Baltimore Orioles began a trading binge that ended fifteen days later. In all, seventeen players were involved in one of the most massive trades in baseball history. The Yankees received pitchers Don Larsen, Bob Turley, Mike Blyzka. They also obtained catcher Darrell Johnson; first baseman Dick Kryhoski; shortstop Billy Hunter and outfielder Tim Fridley and Ted del Guercio. Baltimore obtained pitchers Harry Byrd, Jim McDonald, Bill Miller; catchers Gus Triandos and Hal Smith, second baseman Don Leppert; third baseman Kal Segrist; shortstop Willy Miranda and outfielder Gene Woodling.

November 19, 1921—Three time National League Most Valuable Player Roy Campanella was born in Philadelphia.

November 19, 1951—On his birthday, Roy Campanella of the Brooklyn Dodgers, was voted the National League's Most Valuable Player award.

November 20, 1969—Pele excited the world of soccer and especially his Brazilian countrymen by scoring his 1,000th goal in a game played in Rio de Janeiro.

November 21, 1920—Stan Musial was born in Donora, Pennsylvania. He would go on to star for the St. Louis Cardinals, to win seven batting titles, to record three Most Valuable Player awards and to be admitted to baseball's Hall of Fame.

November 21, 1925—Red Grange performed in his final game for the University of Illinois football team.

November 21, 1931—USC defeated Notre Dame, 16–14. It was the first football defeat in three years for the "Fighting Irish."

November 21, 1934—The New York Yankees purchased Joe DiMaggio from San Francisco of the Pacific Coast League. July 4, 1939—Lou Gehrig's Yankee uniform was the first to be retired. The ceremony took place before a capacity crowd at Yankee Stadium on Lou Gehrig Day.

November 21, 1944—Earl "the Pearl" Monroe was born in Philadelphia. He would become the top draft choice of the Baltimore Bullets in 1967 and win the Rookie of the Year award and go on to become one of the most exciting players in the history of the National Basketball Association.

November 21, 1958—Baseball Hall of Famer Mel Ott was killed in an automobile cash in New Orleans, Louisiana. He was 49-years-old.

November 21, 1959—The inter-league trading ban in baseball was lifted. Two trades were completed on the first day that players were first able to be traded from one league to another. The Cubs traded outfielder Jim Marshall and pitcher Dave Hillman to the Boston Red Sox for first baseman Dick Gernert. The second trade involved the Reds and the A's. Cincinnati sent pitcher Tom Acker to the A's for catcher Frank House.

November 22, 1910—The golf club's steel shaft was patented by Arthur Knight.

November 22, 1917—The National Hockey League was organized in Montreal, Canada. Delegates representing the Montreal Canadiens, Montreal Wanderers, Ottawa and Quebec were present at the organizing meeting. These four clubs together with the Toronto Arenas were admitted into the League. Quebec decided not to compete in the 1917–1918, first season of the NHL.

November 22, 1925—A day after he played his last college game, Red Grange was signed to a professional football contract by the Chicago Bears.

November 22, 1943—Billie Jean King was born. She would become one of the top tennis players in the world and be responsible for many first in the sport. Ms. King would become the first woman to sign a professional contract with a woman's tournament group, the first woman athlete to exceed $100,000 in prize money, the first woman to triumph over a man in a challenge match. Her defeat of Bobby Riggs in 1973 was a boost for women's tennis.

November 22, 1947—The St. Louis Browns received almost $400,000 by selling seven players to three American League teams.

November 22, 1950—Ft. Wayne defeated Minneapolis, 19–18, in the lowest scoring game in the history of the National Basketball Association.

November 22, 1957—A vote taken by the Baseball Writers Association named Mickey Mantle of the New York Yankees the Most Valuable Player over Boston's Ted Williams. The vote caused much dispute and controversy. One of the writers listed Williams ninth: another writer listed Williams tenth on his ballot. These votes made it almost impossible for Williams to win the MVP. However, Williams was named MVP by the "Sporting News."

November 22, 1959—The first draft in American Football League history took place. The first round choices were: Boston: Gerhard Schwedes; Buffalo: Richie Lucas; Dallas: Don Meredith; Denver: Roger LeClerc; Houston: Billy Cannon; Los Angeles: Monty Stickles; Minneapolis: Dale Hackbart; New York: George Izo.

November 23, 1947—The first interracial football game ever staged in the South ended in a 6–6 tie. The occasion was the Piedmont Tobacco Bowl that pitted Washington's Willow Tree Athletic Club, a black team, against the Vulpine Athletic Club of Philadelphia. The game was played at Durham, North Carolina before an integrated crowd.

November 23, 1962—Kelso became a three-time winner of the Horse of the Year award.

November 24, 1960—Wilt Chamberlain pulled down fifty-five rebounds in a game against the Boston Celtics to set an NBA record.

November 24, 1969—Penn State won the Lambert Trophy as the top Eastern football team for the third consecutive year. The 1969 Penn State team won all of its ten scheduled games.

November 24, 1973—In one of sport's most unusual moments, an Oklahoma State guard jumped off the bench to tackle Iowa State quarterback, Buccy Hardeman, who was running for a touchdown. The tackle made by S.L. Stephens, was in vain. Officials ruled that Hardeman would have scored the touchdown. Iowa State won the game 28-12 before an appreciative audience at Ames, Iowa.

November 25, 1874—Joe Gans was born. He would become the first black lightweight boxing champion of the world.

November 25, 1914—The man they would call "the Yankee Clipper" was born in Martinez, California. Joe DiMaggio played sixteen seasons for the New York Yankees, compiled a .325 batting average and a .579 slugging percentage. His great strength was his grace under pressure and an ability time after time to come through with key plays in crucial situations. Three times he won the American League's Most Valuable Player award.

November 25, 1920—Radio's first football game play-by-play took place. The transmission was over WTAW (College Station, Texas). The game pitted the Texas Aggies against Texas U.

November 25, 1944—Judge Kenesaw Mountain Landis died. He had served as Commissioner of Major League baseball for almost twenty-four years.

November 26, 1972—Carlton Fisk, Boston Red Sox catcher, was the first unanimous choice for American League "Rookie of the Year." Fisk smashed 22 home runs, batted .293 and drove in 61 runs.

November 26, 1973—Arthur Ashe became the first black to compete in the finals of the South African Tennis Championship. Ashe was beaten by Jimmy Connors for the championship staged in Johannesburg, South Africa.

November 27, 1926—Army and Navy played to a 21–21 tie at Chicago's Soldier Field. The attendance of 110,000 was the highest in the history of football at that point in time.

November 27, 1947—Joe DiMaggio edged Ted Williams by one vote to win the Most Valuable Player award.

November 28, 1929—For the first time in history, one player scored all of his team's points in a football game. Ernie Nevers of the Chicago Cardinals recorded forty points in his team's triumph over the Chicago Bears.

November 28, 1939—Dr. James Naismith, the man who founded the sport of basketball, died. Nearly fifty years before, he had begun the sport by supervising the first game of the YMCA in Springfield, Mass.

November 28, 1942—Less than 10,000 witnessed the Army-Navy football game. The small attendance was influenced by war time conditions and a presidential decree restricting ticket sales for the game to those who lived within a ten-mile radius of the Annapolis, Maryland playing site.

November 29, 1890—The first Army-Navy football game was played. Navy triumphed, 24–0, despite the fact that the game was played at West Point.

November 29, 1974—James J. Braddock died. In 1935, he pulled a stunning upset defeating Max Baer for the heavyweight championship of the world. In 1937, he lost his title to Joe Louis.

November 30, 1948—The Negro National League disbanded. Officials claimed that the breaking of baseball's color line by Jackie Robinson had made their reason for being no longer feasible. The ten-team Negro American League, however, continued operations.

November 30, 1959—Joe Foss, former Governor of South Dakota, was named American Football League commissioner for a three-year term.

DECEMBER

December 1, 1945—Army's football team concluded its second straight unbeaten season. The Cadets defeated Navy, 32–13. President Harry S. Truman was among the 102,000 that attended the game.

December 1, 1973—Jack Nicklaus became golf's first $2 million career earner. Nicklaus won the Walt Disney World Open tournament to reach that mark.

December 1, 1975—Nellie Fox died. A former star infielder for the Chicago White Sox, he was voted the American League's Most Valuable Player in 1959.

December 2, 1903—Welsh rugby player James Sullivan was born. One of the greatest performers in the history of the sport, Sullivan averaged over a 100 goals a year for nineteen years.

December 2, 1950—The most knockdowns in a title fight took place in a world bantamweight bout at Johannesburg. Vic Toweel knocked Danny O'Sullivan down fourteen times in ten rounds. O'Sullivan retired after the fight.

December 3, 1926—Mickey Walker won a ten round decision over Tiger Flowers and became the new middleweight champion of the world. In 1931, Walker gave up his title and no generally recognized champ arose for a decade until Tony Zale won a fifteen-round decision over Georgie Abrams.

December 3, 1963—The San Francisco Giants traded catcher Ed Bailey, outfielder Felipe Alou and pitcher Billy Hoeft to the Milwaukee Braves for catcher Del Crandall and pitchers Bob Shaw and Bob Hendley. Ernie Bowman also went to Milwaukee later as part of the same deal.

December 3, 1973—Major League baseball adopted a rule that gave umpires permission to state a pitch was a spitball even though they might not be able to detect any foreign substance on the ball.

December 4, 1947—Russia established its eligibility for the 1948 Olympic Games by becoming a member of the International Amateur Union.

December 5, 1908—For the first time in history, numerals appeared on football uniforms. Players on the University of Pittsburgh wore the numbers in a contest against Washington and Jefferson University.

December 5, 1951—Shoeless Joe Jackson died at the age of 64 in Greenville, South Carolina. He played in the major leagues for the Philadelphia

A's, Cleveland Indians and Chicago White Sox.
His lifetime batting average was .356, third
highest in baseball history. He will forever be remembered as one of the eight White Sox players
of 1919 accused of throwing the World Series.
On the lighter side, Jackson was an illiterate hill-
billy who played most of his baseball before he
came to the majors without benefit of spikes or
shoes—and that's how his nickname came to be.
It was suggested that he was the model for Joe
Hardy of Hannibal, Mo., the main character in
the play *Damn Yankees*.

December 6, 1955—Honus Wagner died in
Carnegie, Pennsylvania. A member of the Pittsburgh Pirates for twenty-one years, Wagner won
eight batting titles, collected 3,430 hits and established all kinds of Pirate team records. Five
times he led the National League in stolen bases
while recording a career total of 722. He was admitted to the Hall of Fame in 1936.

December 6, 1969—The governor of Pennsylvania protested the presentation of a plaque by
President Nixon to the University of Texas football team. The plaque proclaimed Texas the top
collegiate team in the United States. Penn State
had won 30 games over the past three seasons.

December 7, 1935—One of football's most unusual days took place as all the points for both
teams in one game were scored by the same
player. University of Washington halfback Byron
Haines scored a touchdown. He was also pushed
over the goal line for a safety giving Southern
California its only points in the game.

December 7, 1941—On this day of the Japanese attack on Pearl Harbor, 43,425 fans were in Wrigley Field in Chicago to watch the Bears play the Green Bay Packers in a National Football League divisional playoff game. At halftime, news of the Japanese attack reached the press box. The Bears won the game, 33–14.

December 7, 1947—Johnny Bench was born in Oklahoma City, Oklahoma. Nineteen years later he would begin his major league career as a catcher for the Cincinnati Reds.

December 7, 1962—Bobo Newsome died in Orlando, Florida. Winner of 211 games, loser of 222, Newsome began his major league pitching career with the Brooklyn Dodgers in 1929 and concluded it with the Philadelphia A's in 1953. In between he played for many different teams.

December 7, 1963—Televising an Army-Navy football game, CBS used "instant replay" for the first time.

December 7, 1973—The San Francisco Giants sold one of their top pitchers, Juan Marichal, to the Boston Red Sox. Marichal was at the tail end of a fine career.

December 8, 1949—Marion Ladewig won an all-star tournament in Chicago and claimed the distinction of being the first official woman bowling champion.

December 8, 1961—One of the most spectacular "shoot outs" in National Basketball Association history took place. The Philadelphia Warriors with Wilt Chamberlain hooked up against the Los Angeles Lakers with Elgin Baylor and Jerry West. At the half—Chamberlain had popped in 28 points to the delight of the hometown Philly fans; Baylor had tallied 16. The game was tied at the end of regulation time and went into overtime. Chamberlain had scored 53 points and Baylor had racked up 47. The game finally ended after three overtimes with Philadelphia a 151– 147 winner. Wilt Chamberlain had broken Baylor's NBA record of 73 points by scoring 78 points; Chamberlain also took 62 shots and made 31 field goals—both NBA game records. Baylor had scored 63 points—but Chamberlain proved the Philadelphia margin of victory.

December 9, 1926—Golf clubs containing steel shafts were approved by the United States Golf Association.

December 9, 1955—A victory over Bobo Olson enabled Sugar Ray Robinson to reclaim for the second time the middleweight boxing title.

December 10, 1810—The first interracial championship fight in history took place. Tom Molineaux, an American black, lost his bid for the heavyweight championship in the fortieth round as Tom Cribb was the victor in their bout at Copthall Common, England.

December 10, 1896—New Haven, Connecticut was the site of the first intercollegiate basketball game. Wesleyan University defeated Yale, 4–3.

December 10, 1946—Hall of Fame pitcher Walter Johnson died in Washington, D.C. He led the majors twelve of his twenty-one years in strikeouts, notching a record 3,508. He pitched 113 shutout games, including a string of fifty-six straight scoreless innings from April 10 to May 14, 1913. He was nicknamed "The Big Train." Part of the reason for the nickname was the seven shutouts he pitched in seven opening day outings which moved his Washington Senators teammates off the track.

December 10, 1971—One of the worst trades in the history of the New York Mets was completed. Nolan Ryan was shipped to the California Angels along with another pitcher, Don Rose, catcher Francisco Estrada and outfielder Leroy Stanton. The Mets received infielder Jim Fregosi. Ryan went on to become one of baseball's most outstanding pitchers.

December 11, 1947—An application by the Pacific Coast League to become a third major league was rejected by the National and American League.

December 11, 1951—The official retirement from baseball of Joe DiMaggio was announced.

December 11, 1973—Houston outfielder Cesar Cedeno was jailed for the alleged shooting death of a 19-year-old woman in the Dominican Republic.

December 12, 1899—The golf tee was patented by George Grant.

December 13, 1924—Larry Doby was born in Camden, South Carolina. He would become the first black player in the American League, the first of his race to win an AL home run title and batting championship.

December 13, 1944—Jockey Edward Garrison died. The term "Garrison Finish" came into the language as a result of his riding technique. Throughout Garrison's long and successful career, he made it a practice to come from behind with a stretch run in the last furlong—a "Garrison Finish."

December 13, 1973—The first franchise granted by the World Football League was given to Detroit.

December 14, 1939—Ernie Davis was born. He would star in football at Syracuse and in 1961 become the first black to win the Heisman Trophy.

December 15, 1950—A one year record for winnings for women's professional golfers was set by Babe Didrickson Zaharias. She won six top tournaments and $14,800.

December 15, 1966—New Orleans became the National Football League's sixteenth franchise.

December 15, 1968—Former heavyweight boxing champion of the world, Jess Willard, died at the age of 87.

December 16, 1966—Dick Tiger won the light-heavyweight championship of the world with a fifteen round decision over Jose Torres.

December 16, 1972—A win over the Baltimore Colts gave the Miami Dolphins the distinction of being the first National Football League team to go through a fourteen-game season without a tie or a defeat.

December 16, 1973—O.J. Simpson became pro football's first player to gain 2,000 yards rushing. Simpson led his Buffalo Bills team to a 34–14 triumph over the Jets and finished the season with 2,003 yards.

December 17, 1933—The Chicago Bears defeated the New York Giants, 23–21, in the first championship game of the National Football League. The victorious Bears received $210.34 each while each Giants player was awarded $140.22 as the loser's share.

December 17, 1952—Archie Moore won a fifteen-round decision over Joey Maxim and the light-heavyweight championship of the world. In 1960, Moore's title was vacated.

December 18, 1898—Count Gaston de Chasseloup-Laubat set the first recognized land speed record for motor cars—a splendid 39.24

m.p.h. for the measured kilometer—at Acheres, France. Gaston's electric Jeantaud lost power and stalled just as it crossed the finish line.

December 18, 1961—Wilma Rudolph was named Woman Athlete of the Year by the Associated Press for the second straight year.

December 19, 1917—The National Hockey League's first season began. The original members of the league were the Montreal Canadiens, the Montreal Wanderers, the Toronto Arenas, Ottawa and Quebec. Quebec did not operate its franchise until 1919, but Joe Malone, Quebec's best player became a member of the Canadiens. On opening night he scored five goals leading Montreal to a 7–4 victory over Ottawa. Though playing in only twenty games that first NHL season, Malone scored forty-four goals—a scoring streak that has never been equaled. The Wanderers opened their season with a 10–9 triumph over Toronto. That game only drew seven hundred spectators. It was the only win the Wanderers ever managed in the NHL—less than a month later—a fire burned down their arena and they withdrew from the league.

December 19, 1934—Al Kaline was born. Twenty-one years later he would become the youngest player to win a major league batting title. Forty-six years later he would be admitted to baseball's Hall of Fame.

December 19, 1959—Penn State was a 7–0 victor over Alabama in football's first Liberty Bowl.

December 20, 1881—Branch Rickey was born in Stockdale, Ohio. He would invent baseball's farm system and be the man mainly responsible for Jackie Robinson's breaking of baseball's color line.

December 20, 1900—Gabby Hartnett, who would play in the major leagues for two decades, was born in Woonsocket, Rhode Island.

December 20, 1905—Philadelphia Jack O'Brien kayoed Bob Fitzsimmons in the thirteenth round. Nearly eleven years passed before the next light-heavyweight title fight.

December 20, 1926—Rogers Hornsby, player-manager of the world champion St. Louis Cardinals, was traded to the New York Giants for second baseman Frankie Frisch and pitcher Jimmy Ring. Hornsby had demanded a three-year contract at $50,000 a year. Owner Sam Breadon refused; the Cardinal owner was also a bit miffed at Hornsby who earlier in the year had thrown him out of the Cardinal clubhouse.

December 20, 1942—Bob Hayes was born. He would win the gold medal in the 100-meter race in the 1964 Olympics, claim the title of the world's fastest human, and go on to star as a member of the Dallas Cowboys football team.

December 20, 1972—Hall of Famer Gabby Hartnett died on his 72nd birthday in Park Ridge, Illinois.

December 21, 1911—Josh Gibson was born. His home run hitting exploits in baseball's Negro Leagues would earn him the nickname "the Black Babe Ruth."

December 21, 1978—Willard Mullin died. He was one of the most famous of all sports cartoonists. His greatest fame came from his creation of the "Brooklyn Bum"—a caricature of the loyal fan who rooted for the Brooklyn Dodgers.

December 22, 1948—Steve Garvey was born in Tampa, Florida. Twenty years later he was playing at Ogden, a minor league farm team of the Los Angeles Dodgers, the teams #1 selection in the 1968 draft. A fixture at first base today for the Dodgers, Garvey is one of baseball's most consistent performers.

December 22, 1973—Dewey Brown died. He joined the Professional Golfers' Association in 1925 and was that organization's first black member.

December 23, 1862—Connie Mack was born. He was the manager of the Philadelphia Athletics baseball team for nearly half a century.

December 23, 1943—Jerry Koosman was born in Appleton, Minnesota. Twenty-four years later he appeared in his first major league game as a pitcher for the New York Mets.

December 23, 1962—One of the longest professional football games ever played took place.

The Dallas Texans defeated Houston, 20–17, in the American Football League championship game. The winning score came on a 25-yard field goal by Tommy Brooker in the 17th minute and 54th second of sudden death. The duration of the game was 77 minutes, 54 seconds.

December 24, 1965—Margaret Curtis died. Ms. Curtis and her sister, Harriot, were excellent golfers. In 1932, they presented the Curtis Cup for competition. Teams of women golfers representing each country compete annually for the cup, with the site alternating between Great Britain and the United States.

December 25, 1971—Professional football's longest game came to an end after 82 minutes and 40 seconds. Garo Yepremian's field goal gave the Miami Dolphins a 24–24 triumph over the Kansas City Chiefs in the second quarter of sudden death.

December 26, 1908—The first in a long line of great black heavyweight champions was crowned. Jack Johnson defeated Tommy Burns to become the first of his race to become heavyweight champion of the world.

December 26, 1941—In his pro tennis debut, Bobby Riggs triumphed over the world champion Frederick Perry.

December 26, 1947—Carlton Fisk, who would star as a Boston Red Sox catcher, was born.

December 26, 1963—Gorgeous George died. His real name was Raymond Wagner. His bleached blond hair and strange ways in the wrestling ring during the 1950s made him a very successful television attraction. Wagner's show business personality and ring antics helped him earn more than $250,000 per annum during his better years.

December 27, 1947—Glenn Davis, who starred for the Army football team, had his application to resign his lieutenant commission turned down by the U.S. Army. Davis had wanted to leave the service in order to be able to play professional football.

December 28, 1902—Pro football's first indoor game was staged at Madison Square Garden. Syracuse defeated Philadelphia, 6–0.

December 28, 1958—Baltimore defeated the New York Giants 23–17 after eight minutes of a sudden-death overtime to win the National Football League championship game. The contest is viewed by many as the greatest football game ever played.

December 28, 1978—Janet Smith won $1.25 million—the biggest soccer pool prize won by one person in history. Ms. Smith forecast all eight ties in English soccer games played the Saturday before.

December 29, 1934—College basketball became big-time. In the first regularly scheduled doubleheader at New York City's Madison Square Garden, New York University defeated Notre Dame, 25–18; Westminster trimmed St. John's, 37–33. A crowd of 16,188 witnessed the doubleheader and "Garden basketball" showcased the best collegiate teams from that point on.

December 30, 1935—Sandy Koufax was born in Brooklyn, New York. Three times he would win the Cy Young Award; four times he pitched no-hitters; five times he led the National League in ERA. In 1971, the man many call the greatest pitcher the Dodgers ever had, was admitted to the Hall of Fame.

December 31, 1961—Green Bay won its first National Football League championship since 1944 by defeating the New York Giants, 37–0, at Green Bay. It was the first million dollar gate in pro football history.

December 31, 1972—Roberto Clemente, on a mission of mercy to supply food and medical supplies to flood victims in Nicaragua, died in a plane crash. The Pittsburgh Pirate outfielder had a .317 career batting average.

ABOUT THE AUTHOR

Harvey Frommer is a professor of journalism, a native New Yorker and student of sports. This is his eighth sports book. Myrna Frommer teaches speech at the City University of New York. This is her first book.